Glimpses of the History of a Bedfordshire Village [Harrold]. Being the substance of lectures, etc.

William Steward

Glimpses of the History of a Bedfordshire Village [Harrold]. Being the substance of lectures, etc.

Steward, William
British Library, Historical Print Editions
British Library
1898
140 p. ; 8°.
10360.e.38.

The BiblioLife Network

This project was made possible in part by the BiblioLife Network (BLN), a project aimed at addressing some of the huge challenges facing book preservationists around the world. The BLN includes libraries, library networks, archives, subject matter experts, online communities and library service providers. We believe every book ever published should be available as a high-quality print reproduction; printed on- demand anywhere in the world. This insures the ongoing accessibility of the content and helps generate sustainable revenue for the libraries and organizations that work to preserve these important materials.

The following book is in the "public domain" and represents an authentic reproduction of the text as printed by the original publisher. While we have attempted to accurately maintain the integrity of the original work, there are sometimes problems with the original book or micro-film from which the books were digitized. This can result in minor errors in reproduction. Possible imperfections include missing and blurred pages, poor pictures, markings and other reproduction issues beyond our control. Because this work is culturally important, we have made it available as part of our commitment to protecting, preserving, and promoting the world's literature.

GUIDE TO FOLD-OUTS, MAPS and OVERSIZED IMAGES

In an online database, page images do not need to conform to the size restrictions found in a printed book. When converting these images back into a printed bound book, the page sizes are standardized in ways that maintain the detail of the original. For large images, such as fold-out maps, the original page image is split into two or more pages.

Guidelines used to determine the split of oversize pages:

• Some images are split vertically; large images require vertical and horizontal splits.
• For horizontal splits, the content is split left to right.
• For vertical splits, the content is split from top to bottom.
• For both vertical and horizontal splits, the image is processed from top left to bottom right.

✝

VIEW IN "HIGH" STREET.

Photo by W. R. Fairey, Harrold.

WILLIAM

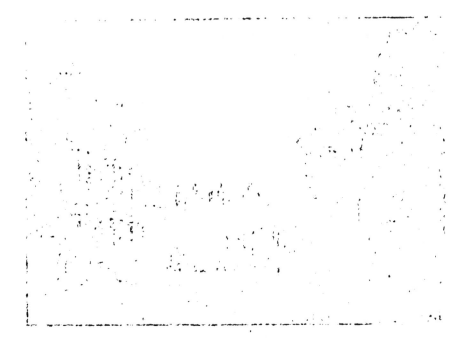

"High" Street.

GLIMPSES
OF THE HISTORY

OF

𝕬 𝕭𝖊𝖉𝖋𝖔𝖗𝖉𝖘𝖍𝖎𝖗𝖊 𝕭𝖎𝖑𝖑𝖆𝖌𝖊

Being the SUBSTANCE *of* LECTURES

DELIVERED AT

HARROLD MUTUAL IMPROVEMENT SOCIETY

1897-98

BY

WILLIAM STEWARD

Bedford :

Printed and Published by the Beds. Publishing Co.
22, Mill Street

MDCCCXCVIII

Contents.

Preface.

THE Village of Harrold is situated about nine miles north-west of Bedford. It is one of a group of villages that lie in the river plain. These river-side villages are probably of great antiquity; in the earliest times primitive families would naturally establish themselves near the river, so as to be able to get water readily and catch fish.

The chief points of interest about the village, besides the church, are the market-place or shelter on the green; the round-house, an ancient structure, probably Saxon or Norman, in which offenders were kept in durance; the bridge over the river, and the causeway. No other village that I know of has so many footpaths radiating around, and you get delightful views of the country from Chellington Hill, from Cracknee Hill, and from Brook Lane, as you go up to the wood. The causeway extends for nearly three hundred yards along the Carlton-road.

As it stands six feet above the roadway, and averages ten feet wide, it serves in fine weather as a very pleasant promenade.

Let me say that I am no antiquarian, and that I entered upon this quest rather accidentally. Having given a lecture before the Harrold Mutual Improvement Society, on PRE-HISTORIC HARROLD, many of the people expressed a desire that I would follow on and say something about Historic Harrold, and, thus, as the shopkeeper in Molière had been talking prose all his life without knowing it, I became an historian in a small way without intending it.

I am not sorry though, now, that I undertook the task; there is nothing like having some one leading subject of inquiry before the mind; from that as a sort of centre you have to go, exploring now in one direction, now in another, and thus you gather in stores of information that you would have acquired in no other way. Through having had to look up the history of Harrold, I know more now about coins, about Roman colonisation, and more especially about mediæval village life, than I ever knew before, or in all probability ever should have known. Writing is not my trade, but every man we say should have a hobby of some sort. This for the last two or three years has been mine.

My sincere thanks are due to Mr. J. S. Phillpotts, M.A., the Headmaster of the Grammar School at Bedford, and to Mr. Clifford Gore Chambers, M.A., the classical master, for their kindness in translating for me the inscription on the Roman Seal, and the passages relating to Harrold in the Hundred Rolls; also to Mrs. Orlebar, of Hinwick, who so kindly placed before me their family records; and Mr. C. Stimson, who read over with me and corrected the sections relating to Feudal Times.

W. S.

Kempston Road, Bedford,
  October 4, 1898.

FOOTPRINTS OF THE ROMANS AND SAXONS.

Footprints of the Romans and Saxons.

ON a former occasion I took for my theme "Pre-historic Harrold," Harrold before history, before men had learned to write, and so transmit their thoughts and the record of events to succeeding generations.

Perhaps I ought not to have given my lecture a local heading, as my remarks referred necessarily to the Ouse Valley here generally, rather than to any particular part of it ; all the same I hope it was not altogether irrelevant to say something about that marvellous structure on which the fleeting habitations, which collectively we call the village of Harrold, are reared. It is interesting to learn, from ancient documents, that certain distinguished families dwelt here centuries ago, but it should be equally interesting to us, from the equally sure evidence of their remains, to learn that the lion and the elephant once roamed over this valley, whilst the hippopotamus wallowed in the river; that there were primitive men hereabouts ages before the earliest recorded races of men, Saxons, Britons, and Iberians had become differentiated from the original stock; that the limestone underlying the turf, and of which so many of your houses are built, proclaim that over here where we now stand, once rolled the billows of the sea; that the very stones about our feet, to him who hath ears to hear, tell a story compared with which the tale of Aladdin's lamp is trivial and commonplace.

From pre-historic we go on now to historic Harrold; to-night we come nearer home and our own times. As well as I could I have told you nature's story. Now for a short time we turn to the records of men.

Until quite lately I was not aware that so many Roman coins had been found here at a farm just outside. By kind permission of Mr. Pickering and the Rev. J. Steel, I had an opportunity of looking over them. There are about forty in all, representing various Roman emperors, Vespasian, Constantine, and others down to Arcadius. They all belong to the period of the Roman occupation of Britain, hence the inference seems unavoidable that there must have been a Roman station here. With the coins was a rectangular seal, with a Latin inscription on two sides of it, setting forth that Caius Junius Tertullus prepared a salve for sore or bleared eyes. I propose to give this inscription presently, and also to go over the coins in order, but first let us try to set before our minds a picture of Harrold, or rather the cluster of habitations which represented our village of Harrold, when the Romans first came this way.

Could you, like some wandering adventurous spirit, have looked around here about 1800 years ago, instead of stone or brick built houses, with gardens near planted with flowers, and meadows beyond bordered by hedges, you would have seen an expanse of forest, of which Odell wood, Dungee wood, and Harrold wood may, perhaps, be regarded as surviving remnants. This forest was the haunt of the wolf, the wild boar, and more rarely of the bear. So much forest favoured dampness; consequently the low grounds generally were swampy. Along most of its course the river was fringed with trees and bushes; here and there a dam, the work of beavers, crossed the stream.

The village you would have found not far from

where it is now, in a glade or clearing. It consisted of an irregular cluster or succession of circular huts, in shape very much like the round-house on the green yonder. These huts were made by driving stakes into the ground so as to form a circle ; from the tops of these stakes other stakes slanted upwards to a centre, forming a conical roof ; the upright encircling stakes were afterwards interlaced with boughs, the roof thatched with flags and rushes.

The people living in these habitations were Celts, and spoke Welsh, or a language allied to the Welsh. Their clothing was made of a coarse home-made felt, worked in glaring colours, for though rude, these people were vain. Pliny says that their garments were striped with little squares of all bright colours, the favourite colour being a flaming red. The dyes for these colours they prepared from the bark of trees, lichens, and other vegetable growths.

Such were the Harroldians of 1800 years ago. As the Romans came to Britain to stay, besides fortified cities and camps, they required forts or stations for the levying and collecting of the tribute, and as abodes for their officials and representatives. One of these stations, we gather from the coins and other relics, must have been here for at least 300 years—a very long period of time, which we shall perhaps better conceive if we recollect that 300 years ago the Spanish Armada had just been defeated, and good Queen Bess was the sovereign of these realms.*

We are not to suppose that the Romans came and conquered Britain for the mere glory of conquering it; they could not afford to do so. To bring 50,000 soldiers in such ships as they had then was a very hazardous and costly enterprise. No. They conquered Britain as we since have conquered India, and were impelled by much the same motive, the hope of gain. In Somersetshire, some time ago, an ingot of lead was found, which, by the date on it in Roman characters, was smelted the year after the first invasion of Claudius. So we see the kind of glory some of them were seeking.

But if the Romans did not come here for the mere glory of the thing, so neither did they interfere much

---

*Pavenham, I am told, owes some of the carvings in the church there to the Spanish Armada. Several of the Spanish ships were driven ashore and part of the wood, it is said, was afterwards cut up and carved into Tritons, Nereids, and other figures for the embellishment of the interior of the Temple Church in London. Seventy or eighty years ago, when the Temple Church was renovated, some of these carvings were taken out, and, according to report, were purchased by Thomas Abbott Green, who placed them in Pavenham Church.

with native customs, or make their rule unnecessarily oppressive. Their practice was to levy a kind of district rate, and appoint local officers to collect it. These officers, natives probably, chosen in each district from among the more influential villagers, received a percentage of the rate, and later on were invested with magisterial powers. I want you to bear this arrangement in mind, as it probably explains the precedence of Harrold in the division or hundred to which in after times it belonged. The reason why the invaders fixed on this particular site for their station is pretty evident. From the slope where these things were found, you can see, as you cast your eye around, the spires of six churches. The Romans, as they advanced, extending their dominion, were careful always to establish themselves where they could get a commanding view of the surrounding country. From this spot they could overlook not only the spreading valley below, but also the winding river, wider then than now, and which, in the absence of roads, was the principal highway.

How large this station was or of what materials it was built we cannot say; probably it was not very large, and it may have been of wood, though as a rule the Romans preferred building with something more solid and lasting. But even if it was of stone it is not to be wondered at if in after time the stones got taken away and used for other purposes.

The Roman rate or tribute was divided into two, tributum or property tax, and annonia, a fixed supply of corn for the Roman soldiers. In villages the rate would necessarily be almost entirely in the form of produce. Even in towns and for long after the Roman period the contributions to the state were part in money and part in produce. Chester we read paid £45 a year and three bundles of martens' skins, Oxford £20 and six measures of honey, Dunchurch £50 and 60,000 herrings. In some cases the tribute was paid in eels. This seems to throw some light on that passage in Domesday, where we read that among its other products or effects Harrold yielded annually 200 eels.

It is significant that though so many Roman coins have been found at this presumed station, none, so far as I am aware, have been found in the village itself. This seems to favour the supposition that money was little known in the village, and that the villagers paid their rate in produce of some kind. This would have to be taken to the station which no doubt served as a depot, not for Harrold only, but for the division round about, a division coinciding approximately most likely with the hundred of later Saxon times.

The earliest coin found here up to the present bears the image and superscription of Vespasian. He was one of the very ablest of Roman Emperors and is said to have built the Coliseum. He became Emperor in the year A.D. 70, the year that Jerusalem was destroyed by his son Titus, and about three years after the death of St. Paul.

Next we have three coins of Antoninus Pius, two silver and one bronze. This Emperor was surnamed Pius because he was of so estimable and virtuous a disposition. He extended the Roman dominion in Britain and re-built the famous wall across from the Tyne to the Solway Firth. This wall, as you know, was intended to keep back the wild Picts from ravaging the southern provinces, which, under Roman rule, were getting more settled and productive.

The next coin in order of time is one of Faustina, the wife of Marcus Aurelius, an Emperor distinguished equally as a philosopher and moralist. Next after this is one of Claudius Gothicus, the scourge of the Goths, and then we come to one of

Carausias. Carausias commanded the legions in Britain and was by them proclaimed Emperor. The Romans had a mint at St. Albans, then called Verulamium, so no doubt this coin was struck there as were most likely several of the others.

Following this we have a coin of Galerius Maximian, and one each of Constantius and Helena his wife, the father and mother of Constantine the Great. This Empress, Helena, is enrolled in the Romish calendar among the saints. Under divine guidance she is said to have gone direct to the place where the cross on which Christ was crucified lay buried. This cross, according to tradition, got divided or broken up somehow into innumerable blocks and bits and distributed afterwards among the Romish monasteries and churches throughout the world for the healing, I suppose, of the nations.

Of Constantine we have four coins. He, it is usually said, was the first Roman Emperor to embrace the Christian religion. More correctly, he was the first to make Christianity the religion of the state. Whilst camping out with his army on a certain plain he saw in the heavens, we are told, the sign of a cross with these words underneath, " By this conquer." Ecclesiastical authorities are by no means agreed as to the kind of cross Constantine saw or whether the message was in Latin or Greek. Cardinal Newman, however, assures us that the miracle may be regarded as established.

Of the other coins I will only give the names: Constantine II. and Constans were sons of Constantine. Magnentius was said to have been on his father's side of British birth. Then we have one of Gratian, two of Valentinian, and one of Valeus. Last in the list are two of Arcadius, who died in 408. Soon after, in 409, the Goths invaded the imperial city and the Roman forces were finally withdrawn from Britain.*

More interesting even than the coins is the stamp or seal of the Roman oculist, Tertullus. Quite a shoal of quacks and adventurers seem to have followed in the wake of the Roman army. Britain, no doubt, in those days, was talked about at Rome just as in the early days of some of us, people used to

---

*Since writing the above, coins of several other emperors, Trajan, Gallienus. Tetrichus, junior, and Constantius. the son of Valentinian, have come to light. Coming down to this side of the Conquest, coins have been found in the village of Henry III., Edward II., Edward VI., Henry VIII., Mary, Philip and Mary, Elizabeth (6), Charles I. and II. (several), William and Mary, (one a crown just as it came from the mint), Anne.

talk about California. Every new country is a famous place for getting on and making money. People go and find out they can get on, that is, if they work, and work harder than ever they cared to work at home. Each earthly paradise when we get to it seems to be made of common earth, thorns also and thistles it doth bring forth. Depend upon it, the struggle for life has been much the same in all ages. In ancient Rome trades-people must have felt the pressure of competition as they do in modern London, only in a different way. One can imagine a friend dropping into the little shop of Tertullus, the apothecary and eye-doctor, and accosting him somewhat in this fashion :—

" Well, doctor, haven't seen you for decades. How are you? It is absurd, I know, to ask a doctor how he is, of course you have the secret and can keep always well, or as well as you want to be, but how are you getting on? How is the trade in herbs and salves? Are there many folks wanting lotions now, or have you cured them all, and done yourself out of a job."

" No, friend," replies Tertullus, " I have not cured them all, but there would have to be a good many troubled with eye affections to keep all the doctors busy that we have in Rome now. Why when I opened this little shop here, there were only four of us, and now there are seven, and another I hear is about setting up in the Appian way. We are too thick here, I am sure, simply eating each other up. In fact Italy is too thickly populated altogether. I am seriously thinking of moving off. They tell me there is a good opening for apothecaries in this new country, Britannia."

"Britannia! You never think of going there surely! Why, the people are all barbarians!"

"Yes, I suppose they are uncivilised and simple, but (smiling) perhaps the more likely on that account to seek our aid. It is not the wisest people always, you know, who prove our best customers."

"No, I suppose not. But this Britannia I hear is such a dull place, wrapped in fog when it is not actually raining. Wolves, too, I am told abound there. It is rumoured also that in the recesses of the forests are dragons and monsters, like Polyphemus, whom we read of in Homer. It would be rather awkward, you know, if you came across one of these when he happened to be wanting his supper."

" Yes, no doubt. But I rather think the monsters
are myths. There has been no Polyphemus as yet
found elsewhere than in the pages of Homer. As
to wolves, we have plenty of them in Italy. It is
not so long since a pair of them were killed here in
one of our public streets. Captain Curtius assures
me that the climate of Britannia, this side next to
Gaul, is not at all bad ; he trades with the natives,
you know, for wool and skins, and has kindly offered
to take me with him. There are a good many
Romans there now, in one capacity or another, and
I rather think I shall go."

Let us hope that our friend prospered, if not at
eye-healing, at wool-buying, or better still, perhaps,
he cleared a space of virgin land, where the Lodge
Farm now is, and grew something, In ancient, as
in modern times, the people who emigrated to new
countries would not be always the people most
wanted in new countries. Thousands of smart
young fellows in our day have gone abroad prepared
to physic people, to draw up deeds, or cast up
accounts, and when they have got to their land of
promise, have found it expedient to turn fruit-growers
or hire themselves out to sheep-farmers.

Several of these Roman stamps have been found in

various parts of the country ; they were used by the apothecaries to mark the wax on the top of their pots of ointment.   One is for a skin ointment, and reads: "Ad cicatrices et aspritudines," which means it was for scars and roughnesses.   Another reads: "The diabulanum (that is eye salve) of Tiberius Claudius, the physician, for all complaints of the eyes.   To be used with eggs."   Another found at Bath had an inscription on four sides, and belonged to a physician named Titus Julianus,   He also was an oculist, and professed to have a cure for cataract.

The inscription on this one found here at Harrold is given below.   As I have said before, for the translation of the inscription and also of the passages relating to Harrold in the Hundred Rolls, I am indebted to the Headmaster of the Grammar School, Mr. J. Surtees Phillpotts, M.A., and the Classical Master, Mr. Clifford Gore Chambers, M.A.

Original Inscription	*Full Latin*	*Translation*
C	Caii	of Caius
IVN	Junii	Junius
TERTVLL	Tertullii	Tertullus
DIAMISVS	dia Misyos	The Salve made of Vitriolic earth (probably vitriolised Fuller's earth)

AD	ad	for
CICS	Cicatrices	Scars

On the other side of the Seal—

C	Caii	of Caius
IVN	Junii	Junius
TERTVLL	Tertullii	Tertullus
DIALEPID	Dialepidos	The unguent or lotion made from Copper Floss (scales that fly off from copper in hammering)
AD	ad	for
ASPR	aspritudines	roughnesses
ET	et	and scurf or sore
S ?	scabritiem ?	eyes.

The original Latin, you will notice, is contracted, a sort of short hand, or business Latin of the time. The Latin you see on druggists' drawers is contracted in some such way. It is the same with our coins, the contractions "*fid. def.*" on them, as you know, stand for "*fidei defensor*," defender of the faith.

You see advertising is not so modern an invention as we sometimes suppose. On each pot of his ointment this old practitioner set forth its virtues; in every paper we pick up, and alas, even on boards defacing the landscape as we fly past in the train, we read, "Floriline for the teeth and breath," "Try Beecham's Pills, they are worth a guinea a box."

During their occupation of Britain the Romans seem to have mingled or intermarried but little with the people outside the towns. To them the native Britons living in villages were mere barbarians. One can picture them, squads of them, coming from or going to this station just outside; marching through the village, with their steel arms and flashing brazen armour and helmets, the women with feminine curiosity watching them from within the shadow of their primitive homes, whilst the children outside, half shy and half afraid, also eyed them wonderingly as they passed. Little did those world-conquerors then suspect that this obscure island, set, as they imagined, upon the very rim and margin of the world, would one day be the centre of an empire such as Rome, in her meridian glory, hardly dreamed of.

When the Romans withdrew from Britain the natives were in helpless plight. For over 300 years they had not been called on as a nation to defend themselves against outside foes, and now they were unable to defend themselves. It was much the same with the Saxons afterwards when the Danes fell upon them. Fighting is like every other accomplishment; if you are to maintain your proficiency you must practise, keep your hand in.

The German and Scandinavian invaders were less civilised than the Britons whom they supplanted, but they had this in unusual degree—energy; they were men of force, and force moves and rules the world. If a young man is to succeed in the battle of life, whatever else he may have he must have "go." It is so with races. There are nations more artistic, and in other ways more clever than we, but no other European nation has shown equal power, tenacity, and endurance. We have not yet painted a Madonna, it is sometimes said. No, but we have built the steam engine and laid down the railway; and we have done these things, our genius has taken this line, because we are the children of those fierce Vikings, whose great god was Thor, the hammerer. This same initial force—racial inertia—has urged, carried us to the uttermost parts of the earth and made us rulers over an empire on which, as we boast, the sun never sets. "And I perceive now," says Mark Twain, "that the English are mentioned in the Bible. Blessed are the meek, for they shall inherit the earth."

Of the villages, even of the towns, during the Saxon period, we have no separate history. We only know that Harrold and the villages round about, indeed the whole of this part of the country, was peopled by the West Saxons; not without strenuous resistance though, it would seem, from the native Britons. "The men of Kent," says Green, "had been established in their new homes for a century before the West Saxons succeeded in appropriating Bedfordshire."* How do we know that this part of the country was peopled by the West Saxons? We know it by the names of places round about Felmersham, Pavenham, Carlton, and Chellington.

The terminations to these names, "ham" and "ton," have the same signification: They indicate or imply, says Mr. Seebohm, a village with a Manor House, the "gret house," as old-fashioned village folk sometimes call it. They furnish also a clue by which we may find out approximately who the people were who centuries before the Norman

---

*Green's " Making of England," p. 123.

Conquest settled in Harrold and the villages round about.

For these terminations, "ham" and "ton" are peculiar to this south eastern part of the country; they die away as you go north and west. In my own native county, Worcestershire, for instance, I cannot call to mind a single place the name of which ends in "ham," and only one or two in "ton." Instead of these we get the termination "ley": Bendley, Arley, Abberley, Hagley, Trimpley, Wolverley, and many more. This difference in terminations was a peculiarity which struck me when I first came to this part of the country. It must have some historic significance; let us try and find out what it is.

If we go over to Germany we find a region where the termination "ham" or "heim" prevails, even more than with us; it is the region embracing both sides of the upper part of the Rhine—Elsass, Baden, and the country about Frankfort and Mayence. Many tribes we know contributed to the peopling of England in the centuries after the Roman evacuation, Jutes, Angles, Saxons, Danes, and Norsemen. The occurrence of names in this neighbourhood terminating in "ham" and "ton" furnishes something like proof that this part of the country was taken possession of by that branch of the great German family whose home was the region I have indicated. They sailed down the Rhine in their flat-bottomed boats, and the nearest coast as they crossed the channel would be that of Norfolk, Suffolk, and Essex. There they landed, and gradually spread inland, driving the natives before them like sheep. Then, as they settled down here and there, they naturally named their hamlets in the way or by the rule which they had been accustomed to in their native land.

Along the valley from Harrold to Bedford there are nearly a dozen villages, the names of which terminate in " ham " or " ton," Carlton, Chellington, Felmersham, Pavenham, Milton, Steventon, Clapham, Bromham, Biddenham, Goldington, and Newnham.

In some cases a name was suggested by, or retained on account of, some natural peculiarity ; thus we have Sharnbrook and Bedford—the ford of Bedd, or Bedican. The name, Harrold, was likewise suggested most probably by surrounding natural features. The ancient form of the name was Harewold. "Wold," as you are aware, means a wood, or wild uncultivated tract. A mile or two away we have Odell wold—the wold of Odell. This particular district, we may suppose, was for a similar reason called Harewold, the wold of Hare, whoever or whatever Hare may have been.

But these terminations tell us something more important. Felmersham meant the ham, home, or manor of Felmer, and so these terms "ham" and "ton," though partly fossilised now, tell us of a manorial system; in each village a manor house, with a lord of the manor, who was subject to military service, and responsible for the maintenance of order and the administration of justice, the land being culti-vated by semi-servile dependents, who were in fact part and parcel of the estate.

This was, undoubtedly, the social system in this part of the country during the middle ages, and it clings to us still; in the west and north a different order generally prevailed. I spoke just now of the termination, "ley," in Worcestershire; ley, lea, or leigh means grass land—"The lowing herd winds slowly o'er the lea." Towards Wales the tribes were less settled, probably less civilised, and depended rather on their flocks and herds than on the cultivation of the soil.

To get an idea of the place and status of Harrold, in the centuries after the Roman evacuation, it will be necessary to look a little into the administrative

c

machinery of the Anglo-Saxons. The Saxon parliament was called the Witenagemote, or council of wise men. These were mostly thanes, bishops, and representative freeholders. Under the Witenagemote were the folk moots, or shire moots; these were usually presided over by the King. At first the King would go round with his proposed laws to the several shire moots, getting the separate consent of each to his proposals, which he would then submit to the Witenagemote. Beneath the shire moots were the hundred moots, presided over by a lord, or by an elected hundred elder. The hundred comprehended a number of villages, and, according to some authorities, was so called because each such division was expected, if called upon, to furnish a long hundred, that is 120 men, all fully equipped for the wars. Hence the quota of these brave warriors that Harrold itself had to equip and send forth, was about eight.

But this was not all. Harrold, so it appears, was the chief village, a sort of capital of the hundred, just as Bedford was and is of the shire. And so, in time of war, the constable of Harrold had not only to see to the equipment of the Harrold recruits, he had also to call out the levies from the other villages in the hundred, and to see that they also were properly equipped.

HAREWOLD PRIORY

From an Old Print.

One wonders whether this precedence of Harrold in the hundred may be explained partly by these coins. Let us look at the evidence, what there is of it. First, there is the fact of these coins, etc., being found here. From this fact we infer that the Romans had a station here. Where they had stations it was their custom to appoint local officers whom they invested afterwards with magisterial powers. The Saxon period is to us a great gulf. It is generally supposed, though, that the Saxons in arranging their hundreds had regard to the known Roman divisions ; if such was the case there would naturally be a continuity of administrative function in those places where there had been Roman stations. Whether this was so in this particular case we cannot say, simply because during the Saxon period there is no village history ; but it would seem that Harrold must have been a place of some importance because, soon after the Conquest, a priory was founded at Harewold, the only village in the hundred that has ever had any such institution. Later on, near the time of the Commonwealth, we find Sir Samuel Luke writing to the Constable of Harrold, as the Constable of the Willey Hundred, calling on him to get the levies together, to see that they were properly provisioned, and send them on to Bedford. Harrold gave the title of Earl to one of the de Greys, and petty sessions for the hundred, also for the hundreds of Stodden and Barford, were formerly held here.

These, I know, are but glimpses of history; still they suffice to shew the exceptional position of Harrold in the Willey Hundred in feudal times. Beyond the Conquest is the Saxon gulf or deluge, beyond that these coins. May we not conjecture that the pre-eminence of Harrold in feudal times began with this presumed Roman station? In the absence of connecting evidence one can only speculate; yet speculation suggested by these scattered facts will, I hope, be regarded as not altogether idle or unprofitable. In process of time, as landlords in one way or another got relieved from the obligation of rendering military service, the hundred as a political division gradually became obsolete. Harrold then lost its pre-eminence and became an ordinary village, yet still one of the largest villages in the county.

THE VILLAGE IN FEUDAL TIMES

The Village in Feudal Times.

THE first actual mention of Harrold in history is in the famous Domesday book, a book prepared by order of William the Conqueror; a survey in fact of the various villages and estates throughout the country. The passage relating to Harrold reads thus:—

Manor. Judith fee. Honor of Huntingdon. "The land of Countess Judith in Wilga Hundred." "Gilbert de Blosseville holds Harewelle of the Countess and is rated for ten hides. There is land for sixteen plough-teams; in demesne are three plough-lands* and one can be made, and there are ten villeins† with seven plough-lands and other six can be made.

---

*A plough-land was as much land as a plough could plough in a year.

†There were probably other labourers in the village besides these ten villeins   There is no reason to conclude that *Domesday* gives an accurate statement of the whole of the able-bodied population.—See Cunningham's " History of English Industry and Commerce," p. 160.

Pasture for six plough-teams, wood for 200 hogs and a mill of thirty-six shillings and eight pence and 200 eels. The whole worth six pounds, when he received it £16, in the time of King Edward £20. Three thanes of King Edward held this Manor and could sell it to whom they pleased."

This passage may seem obscure and uninteresting, but if we read it carefully we shall get, I think, a very fair idea or picture of the social life of the village in that distant time.

This Gilbert de Blosseville, whose name we find in that of a neighbouring village, Newton Blossomville, was rated, we read, for ten hides. Now a hide of land was 120 acres* so that his ratal was on 1,200 acres. The whole area of Harrold was, and is, 3,200 acres. Consequently we infer that considerably more than half the land then must have been unclaimed waste.

The land then, as now, was divided into arable and pasture. Part of it was demesne or lord's land, part of it held by husbandmen, villeins as they were called. Of these villeins there were ten in Harrold.

---

*A hide, according to some authorities, was only 100 acres, a virgate in some places 20, in others from 24 up to 30 acres.

They were peasant farmers really, in semi-servile subjection to the lord of the Manor. The ordinary holding of a villein was a virgate of land or 30 acres. Each villein also was supposed to have two oxen for ploughing. So you see the ancient rule was not three acres and a cow, but thirty acres and two oxen. Two oxen, of course, were not of much use for ploughing with such ploughs as they had then; so the villeins had to co-operate, help one another. An ordinary plough-team consisted of eight oxen and so they went from one holding to another; at night each villein took his own oxen to his own stall.

But the holding of a villein was a holding and no more; the whole of the land in the village belonged to the lord of the Manor, and not the land only, the cattle, the ploughs, the tools, even the rude furniture of the cottages, all were theoretically the property of the lord, "The *Gebir* had a yardland of thirty or forty acres which, when he entered on it, was stocked with two oxen, and one cow, and six sheep, as well as tools for his work and utensils for his house."* All these were included in the holding and for having this holding to do as he could with,

---

*Cunningham's "History of English Industry and Commerce," p. 102.

the villein had to render to his lordship certain services.

These services were regulated by custom and were different in different counties or localities. Speaking generally, a villein worked four days for himself and two days for the lord, at harvest three days; in winter he had to lie at the lord's fold as often as he was told. Then, too, there were little donations, such as eggs, that at stated periods he had to take to the Manor House. On one estate, in Huntingdonshire, after setting forth what work the villein should do on the lord's land, the deed goes on to say :—

"Also he gives ½ bushel of corn as bensed in winter time ;

" Also ten bushels of oats at Martinmas as fodder corn ;

" Also 1d. on Ash Wednesday as fish-penny ;

" Also 20 eggs at Easter ;

" Also 10 eggs on St. Botolph's day* (in June)."

One can conceive with what feelings people, as they got a little enlightened, came to regard these exactions. What blessings would be showered on Sir Gilbert's head, as the Harrold peasant rose from

---

*Seebohm's " English Village Community."

his wooden bench, his only chair, to look up a score of eggs or seize his best fowl to take up to "the house."

Money, amongst the common people in those days, was very little known. As it became more distributed, and its uses better understood, the lords of the Manors were glad enough to get the grudging doles and services of the villeins commuted to a fixed yearly money payment or rent. The rent was from half a mark (6s. 8d.) to a mark and a half per virgate, and Bedfordshire was one of the first counties to adopt the rule of money payment in lieu of service and doles.

There were ten, we read, of these villeins or husbandmen in Harrold. Strictly speaking they were not slaves; after rendering the required doles and services to the lord, they could own property other than land, and bequeath it to whom they would, but they could not leave the estate on which they were born; if they did they were pursued as fugitives and brought back. If a villein married without the lord's consent he was fined, if he sold an ox without license he was fined, and so he was if his daughter got into trouble.

When a villein died his holding, not the

land, passed to his eldest son. With each holding, as I have said, the lord claimed the customary services and doles, consequently he was opposed to the breaking up of the holding, because it would have confused things. In some such way probably originated the custom of primogeniture.

The successor to a holding had to pay an ox to the lord as heriot* or failing an ox the best thing he had. In this custom again we see the origin of copyhold estate. Nobody could really own land but the lord of the Manor. Even when in later times a villein purchased his holding, it was still subject to heriotage. That is to say it was copyhold rather than freehold.

But if the villeins were not actually slaves there were English slaves in those days. In Odell there were thirteen villeins and five slaves; in Pavenham three slaves; in Steventon two. There were none, however, in Harrold. You see how early our village began to be distinguished for independence and love of freedom.

---

*A *Heriot*, in theory, was the return to the lord of the horse and arms with which the lord had equipped the lately deceased thegn, by the heir who had entered on the estate.—Medley's "Constitutional History."

We speak of the Normans sometimes as robbers: in justice to them let it be said that they did not originate or introduce this manorial or feudal system, they simply found it and fell in with it. The Norman knight took the place of the Saxon thane. In innumerable instances the case, so far as the villeins were concerned, was not for the worse. In Harrold it looks as though the Norman yoke must have been lighter than that of the Saxon. In the time of Edward the Confessor three Saxon thanes took toll here, and the whole property was estimated as worth £20 a year; under Gilbert de Blosseville the returns or yearly value sank to £6.

But neither were the Saxons the authors or originators of the manorial or feudal system. If we want to get at the real beginning of the system we must go back to the time of the Romans. A Roman veteran, who had served in the wars, was usually recompensed by the gift of an estate in one of the conquered provinces. There was no difficulty about finding these estates. Owing to the desolating wars vast tracts in Germany and Central Europe were depopulated. Besides the estate the Roman veteran was furnished with an outfit of seed and cattle, and for labourers he annexed the natives, if there were any, or he purchased slaves, thousands of which, Germans, Franks, Britons, were to be bought at the various marts.

Besides these veterans, numbers of wealthy and noble Romans bought lands of the state, built huts for their slaves, and a villa for themselves, and lived as kings in their little domain, monarchs of all they surveyed. So many were there of these Roman settlements in the part of Germany our forefathers came from, that it became a Roman province called *Germania Prima.**

In process of time the settlers, as is always the case, became naturalised, the native language prevailed, the Roman term, villa, got superseded by the more homely heim, home, or great house. Not though in all cases. Here and there the Roman termination " ville " persisted. Our word village is derived from the Latin villa, and so is villein, which meant originally a husbandman of the village. As the feudal system collapsed, and men became more free and independent, villein became an epithet of contempt and opprobrium.

*The system of cultivation in Britain also during the Roman occupation was manorial, hence it is supposed that in many cases the Saxons simply took possession of, and established themselves in, Manors that they found here.

One volunteer, we often say, is worth two pressed men. This cultivation of their estates by slaves was found not to answer well. The slaves were not of the stuff of which slaves are made; they required much over-seeing and chastisement. No system works well that is not largely self-acting. Weary of watching and beating, the lords of the manors took to allotting equal portions of the land for the slaves to cultivate for themselves, on the understanding that they rendered certain services, and gave part of the produce. This was the point the system had reached in its development in Germany, when the Saxons came over here. This system, which they had been accustomed to, they naturally kept on with in their new country. The Saxon chief, or thane, established himself in the village, and it became his ham or ton. The Normans, when they came, found no fault; the arrangement rather suited their plans; only it was exit Waltheof and the three lesser thanes of Harrold, enter Judith and Gilbert de Blosseville.

Before we pass on let me say a word about the cultivation of land under the manorial system. The ten villeins in Harrold had each a holding of 30 acres, or 300 acres in all. Besides this there was, of course, the demesne land of the lord, which they had to cultivate in lieu of rent, or rather because rent, so far at least as they were concerned, was not then invented.   Now this 300 acres was distributed in three fields, one sown with wheat. one barley—say—or oats, and one fallow.   But each villein's portion was not, as we might suppose, a ten acre plot in each field.   On the contrary, the fields were divided into half acre plots, or strips, the strips being approximately 40 rods long, and two rods wide.   Forty rods, you know, make a furlong, or furrow long, that being the usual distance they ran the furrow before turning.   There were no hedges or permanent fences, the strips were divided by turf balks, like those we see in allotment fields.   Each furrow was supposed to be a foot wide, hence the oxen in ploughing half a rood travelled one furlong, that is 220 yards, eight times.   Eight times 220 yards is a mile, so that in ploughing an acre they went eight miles, which was considered a day's work.   After ploughing there was no harrowing to speak of, or rolling, consequently the crops were very poor.   The average yield of wheat was ten bushels per acre, or about five times the quantity sown as seed.

In ploughing along the side of a hill the plough went back idle; as a consequence the soil was all the while thrown to the right. This, in time, tended to form a flat - topped bank, or a succession of flat topped banks or terraces. An example of this terrace formation can be seen near Luton, as you go by train ; another example you may see in a field at Stevington, as you go by the river from Pavenham. The terraces sweep round in amphitheatral form, and one gentleman, last year, suggested to me that the Romans might have shaped the ground that way for some spectacular display. It is rather a drop from amphitheatres to furrows, but my conviction is that the formation is due to the ancient system of ploughing. Last time I walked that way I stepped across them, and found that one terrace is about two rods wide and the other four.*

Village life in those times, when everybody was subject to the authority of one, must seem to us ignoble and monotonous. No parish councils then, no nonconformity, no going your own way. At eight in the evening the curfew bell rang from the church tower ; put out the light, put out the fire. If, after that time, anyone was seen abroad he was taken to

---

*These terraces are supposed by some to have been the work of the pre-historic Iberians.—See " Gomme's Village Community."

the round-house, and next morning had to appear before Sir Gilbert to give account of himself. If he otherwise misconducted himself he was clapped in the stocks, which were close by the round-house, to endure the jeers and grins of the passers by.

Yet no doubt they had ways of enjoying themselves even in feudal times. It is by no means a sombre picture of society that Piers Plowman draws in his poem. There, in his vision, he sees a fair field, and the woolcomber, the weaver, and all manner of people conversing together, and strolling leisurely about, whilst the ploughman drives his team, and the baker cries " Hote pies, hote."

In this Domesday survey Harrold mill is valued at 36s. 8d. a year, that is about 8½d. per week. This looks pretty cheap, more especially as there were then certain common rights, and most likely some land with it. It looks as though the present tenant might well apply for a return to the original rent. Only there is the difference in the value of money to be thought of. In one of the agreements of that time, we read that a certain tenant, among other contributions, is to give 2d. yearly, or one small sheep. So it seems by that that one small sheep was then worth 2d. Working this out we find that the equivalent of 36s. 8d. was 220 lambs or small sheep; so on the whole the present tenant had perhaps better not raise the question of the original rent.

From Domesday Book also we learn that the manor of Harrold was owned by Judith, the niece of William the Conqueror. Until she refused to marry the man of his choice she was a great favourite with her uncle, who conferred on her, besides the manor of Harrold, many other manors and estates throughout the country. Now there is an element of romance about this lady Judith, and I think I shall be able here to spin out a little love story, to relieve and brighten this, my paper, which, I fear, is getting rather dry and tedious. Nowadays, nearly all literary food needs to be spiced with fiction or romance. Each weekly periodical, each monthly magazine, must entice its readers with a story, the story serving as a bait, a sort of literary jam to be taken with the physic of the teaching, the doctrine, or the history.

Well, this Judith, niece of the Conqueror, and lady of the manor of Harrold, married a great Saxon noble, Waltheof, Earl of Huntingdon, Northampton, and Northumberland. After she had married him she met with someone whom she thought she would like

better (a not unusual circumstance), so she betrayed
her husband to her uncle, who sentenced Waltheof
to death. And now the way seemed open for the
new alliance, but the crafty often get caught in the
net of their own devices.

William had a faithful friend and follower, St.
Simon de Liz, whom he wished to honour and
advance ; so he proposed that his niece, who had
now all the estates of the great Earl Waltheof,
Harrold included, should marry his friend Simon.
This proposal she resolutely declined, whereupon
William threatened her with the sequestration of her
estates. She didn't care, if she married again it
should be a husband of her own choosing. Besides
this Simon was lame and deformed, in ancient phrase
he " halted," and she was not going to have a cripple
for a husband, hobbling about. True to his word,
William deprived her of most of her property. In
those days people sought to atone for their offences
by building churches. Judith, for her sins, founded
the nunnery of Elstow. But if Judith saw no comeli-
ness in Simon, her daughter Maud did, or possibly
she felt sorry and took pity on him, anyway she
married him. Let us hope they lived happily ever
after. From Gilbert de Blosseville the manor of

Harrold passed to John de Grey, who was related by descent to Judith. With this illustrious family it has been associated ever since, right down to the present day.

In the year 1150 Sampson le Fort, said to have been one of the bravest knights of his time, founded a priory at Harewold, for canons and nuns of the order of St. Nicholas of Arrouasia, but it was afterwards occupied by a prioress and nuns of the order of St. Austin. The convent seal was a pointed oval, the device being St. Peter standing with the keys in his right hand, and a cross in his left. The land for the endowment of the priory was in Kent, and yielded a rent of nearly £40 a year. The site of the priory was at the back of the present school-house, near the river, and it stood as a priory for nearly 400 years, till the dissolution of the monasteries, when the site was granted by Henry the Eighth in 1538 to John Cheney Gent, of Pightlesthorpe, Bucks. and Lord Parr, from whom it passed to the De Greys. In whole or in part, however, the building remained for another 300 years, being used mainly as farm buildings or stabling; the last of it, the refectory, was not pulled down till 1840.

HARROLD IN FEUDAL TIMES

Harrold in Feudal Times.

AFTER Domesday, the next source of information about Harrold is the Hundred Rolls,
Rotuli Hundredorum, of the time of Edward the First.
These rolls were prepared, or rather the survey which
is recorded in them was taken with the object of
rectifying certain abuses which, during the turbulent
reign of Henry the Third, and whilst his successor
King Edward the First was engaged in the wars of
the Crusades, had crept into the administration,
"whereby," it was said, "the revenues of the crown
had been seriously diminished, and numerous exactions and oppressions of the people had been committed by the nobility and clergy." The first rolls
were written immediately after the return of Edward
from Palestine. Of the survey made in the seventh
year of his reign, only the rolls relating to Bucking-
hamshire, Cambridgeshire, Huntingdonshire, Oxfordshire, part of Bedfordshire, and two other
counties are now known to be extant. The information given in these rolls, the later ones more

particularly, is much fuller, more detailed, than that given in Domesday. For instance, defining certain boundaries, these documents say that John de Grey has fishing rights along with Ralph Perot and Ralph Morin, "a Budewelle usque ad ponte de Harewold." By this we know that there was a bridge at Harrold over 600 years ago. My conviction is there has been a bridge here for more than twice that time, and probably a causeway as well; but before going into this question let us look in at our village again. We saw what it was like in the time of the Romans, let us see how it looks now after the lapse of a thousand years.

It is the year 1280. John de Grey is lord of the Manor,* with control over the woods, the river (fire and water), and the village stocks, or gallows, for the punishment of thieves; he also has View of Frankpledge,† right of warren, and a principal interest in two water mills.

---

*_Harewold_, John de Grey, Fit in Harewold, ignem & aqam, infongindepef & ceta omnia que spctant, ad coronam eo qot dea villa, est de honor de _Huntyngdone_ cum vis' frncipleg' & aliis ad illud spetantibs & furcas, maxe infa xii annos ultimos elapsos, levata, &c, _Rotuli Hundredorum._—Vol II., p 323.

†_View of Frankpledge._ It was customary for the lord to group his vassals into tythings, or tens, the members of each tything being _pledge_ or surety for one another; then if any

HARROLD BRIDGE FROM THE CAUSEWAY.

Photo by W. R. Fairey Harrold

In Harewold, John de Grey has in demesne three earucates of land, that is about 360 acres. Of this two carucates are arable, thirteen acres meadow and pasture, and 120 acres wood. This land, the arable portion of it, is cultivated by tenants, who give their services in lieu of rent. In return for these services each tenant has a virgate, or half virgate, of land allowed him to cultivate for himself. Besides his holding each tenant has a tenement, for which he pays two shillings a year, "or work to that value." One tenant holds his land rather differently. For his half virgate he pays a rent of half a mark (6s. 8d.) a year, " or work to that value." All the same he is a servile tenant, "inasmuch as he cannot give his daughter in marriage nor sell the produce of his

---

crime or offence was committed he, the lord, could summon any member of the tything or the whole of them ; if he still failed to find out the delinquent, or supposed delinquent, he could fine them all. Twice a year the lists of the tythings were looked over to see if they were complete, and in order; this was the *View* of Frankpledge. The courts were held usually in the open air. In taking oath the person called on placed his hand under his thigh. From the number of Courts it would seem that people must have been governed considerably more then than we are now. This appearing at Court was, to simple people, a very serious business, so in all ordinary affairs the villeins preferred to be represented in the Courts by the great man, the lord of the Manor, who answered and spoke for them. This sponsorship was thought so much of that it was usually included in the terms of the deed or agreement of tenancy.

beasts without license from the lord "—sicut suus ita qd non potest maritar filias suus nec putt s^i pullat vende sine licentia. This tenant, Simon Huntingdon, is of higher dignity than the others; he is a villein, they are only cottiers. Their names are William Ward, Barthelot, William Pekkebene, William Leman, Roger Wylk, Robert Raven, William Ho.

Under the superiority of John de Grey, Richard de Pabenham,[*] of Pavenham, has, in Harewold, four virgates, four acres of arable and pasture land, and twenty acres of enclosed wood. The four acres of land and the twenty acres of wood he holds in demesne, the other he lets at the customary rent, a mark per virgate a year. Three tenants, William Bidun, Henry de Broest^{ate} and John de Broest^{ate}, each holds half a virgate in servile tenancy; two others are free tenants, that is to say, they can marry their daughters, and sell their calves and. young stock, without paying license to the lord. These free tenants are Nicholas Engayne and Robert le Champiun. For his virgate the latter pays, as rent, one pound of pepper and one pound of wax a year, *j virg. p j liba pipis & j lib^a cere p. annum.*

---

*A mistake probably for *John* de Pabenham, who at this time was M.P. for Bedfordshire.

" Richard de Esseby holds, in the same manor of
said John of said honor," three virgates of land, for
which he pays one pound of cumin (cimini) a year.*
With him he has one nief (nativus), Richard Leman,
who rents a cottage from him at twelve pence a year
" or work to that value."

Subject to the same overlordship, the knights
templars of Jerusalem, " of the temple of God and
of Solomon," hold in Harewold, "in free and ever-
lasting alms," 292 acres, the gift in the reign of
King Henry of a certain Flaundrine Manduyt. The
order of knights templars was formed to drive out
the Saracens from Palestine, a task the knights find
to be not an easy one; meanwhile they are supposed
to protect pilgrims on their way to and from the
holy places at Jerusalem. Just now there is diffused,
amongst all classes, a fanatical zeal for Jerusalem,
and an equally fanatical antipathy to the Jews. At
home, surrounded by their serfs, the templars are
monks, but when they go forth they are mail-clad
warriors, rather addicted to display. From the
badge on their right shoulder they are called the red
cross knights. Besides this estate the templars have
properties also at " Hynewic," " Sharnebroc," and

---

*Cumin :—A spice at that time much valued.

two or three other places round about, but they are not thought very much of. Among the people it is rumoured that they practise secret rites and hold strange doctrines; worse than all, many of them are foreigners, so they are regarded with suspicion and disfavour.* Those living here hold, in demesne, three virgates of land, the rest they let to tenants at the usual rent, one mark per virgate per ann. "or work to that value."

As in other cases the tenants are some of them servile, and some free. Of the former, who are slaves till they "ransom their blood," (de sangine suo eund) William Baker, William Ode, Hyllary, and Roger de Cakebroke, each holds half a virgate; and, under the same conditions of servile tenancy, Adam Persun, William Howel, Henry Ketel, and Reginald de Mercer, have each a cottage at a penny, and service. Richard Leman, Walter le Barker, and Ham (Hamlyn ?) de Circestre are free tenants, holding tenements at rents respectively, of twelve pence, eighteen pence, and six pence per annum.

The priory, together with the church, has, as en-

---

*Soon after this time, in the year 1312, the order of Knights Templars was suppressed, and their property transferred, most of it, to the Knights Hospitallers.

dowments, one virgate of land, twenty acres of wood, one carucate of land, containing 120 acres, all in "pure and free alms" (Frankalmoigne).* They also hold three virgates of land, which Ralph Morin gave to the Abbot of Butlesdene in the time of King Henry, at a rent of one pound of pepper a year.

Besides the tenants previously enumerated, Robert Amory holds, of John de Grey, one virgate of land in free marriage; Roger de Boyner, two virgates at a penny; Reginald, son of Reginald, three quarter virgates of land, at six shillings and nine pence, and "suit and for"; Henry son of Hyllary, one virgate at suit of court and for; Richard Curtevalur, one virgate at six pence per annum; Henry de Broestᵃte one virgate at suit of court and for and sixpence a year; William le Flemyng, one virgate at seven shillings and two pence a year; Gilbert, son of Matthew, one virgate at half a mark and for; William Romay, half a virgate at half a mark and for; Robert le Champiun, half a virgate at seven shillings, suit and for; William de Habinton, to Ralph Morin, twenty five pence, remainder to John de Grey, with suit of court and for; John de Montibz, one quarter at two capons a year, suit of court and

---

*Frankalmoigne, free from royal and other claims.

for ; Ralph Ravenleg, one messuage at two shillings a year ; Hugh Cudding, one messuage at a penny a year ; Isabett, daughter of Galf, one messuage at six-pence and suit of court ; Eletnys, one messuage at seven pence a year ; Richard de Broest^ate, one mes-suage at a farthing a year ; Robert Megge and John, son of Walter, one messuage at sixpence and suit ; Richard Druye, one messuage at a penny and for ; Robert le Marescal, one messuage at sixpence. Besides this the Master of the Hospital at Bedford has one messuage, given him in the time of King John, of which William, son of Stephen, is tenant at a rent of two shillings a year.

But although John de Grey is lord of the manor he is not here very often. The Greys have many manors, so John de Grey just now is living at Dun-stable, and the great man of the place is Ralph Morin, whose mansion is near the church. This mansion is a rambling one-storeyed structure, built of local limestones, unhewn and roughly cemented together with clay or mud, and thatched with straw. It extends along one side of a quadrangle, the other sides being occupied by stables, cowsheds, and out-houses. In the middle of the quadrangle is the dunghill, for the time of microbes is not yet come.*

The record of the tenants of John Morin and their holdings, unfortunately, is not complete. Richard the reeve, or constable (prepositus), has one virgate; Robert le Poter, half a virgate. Then William Guyden, and three or four others, have each a cottage at twelve pence, or work to that value. These are servile tenants, villeins, bound to ransom their blood (de sangine sua emendo). Of free tenants we have Robert le Cauncelor and John Morin, also Robert Amory, who holds a virgate in free marriage; William son of Stephen, one virgate at three shillings a year and suit; Isabett Ingeland, and Simon le Neve, one messuage each at twelve pence a year; and Richard Faber, one messuage at fourteen pence a year.

The Mansion, I said, is near the church; it does not follow from this that Ralph Morin is exceptionally devout; he needs to be near the church because the church is not only a sanctuary, it is also the village hall. In time of peace it is the registry office; in time of danger a place of refuge. It is occasionally also a storehouse: there are few barns in the

---

*A clay walled cottage under thatch represents an ancient family mansion of a grand squirearchial race four hundred years ago.—" The Village Community,"—G. L. Gomme, p. 117.

E

village, and so after harvest the people are glad to store wheat, rye, oats and other produce in the church, as, provision for winter. You can even get what is called church ale, for the churchwardens brew ale and sell it in the church for the benefit of the church. Money is much wanted just now, for the church, you see is old and dilapidated, and Sir John wants to get it restored after the new and beautiful style in which so many churches are being restored throughout the country.*

The vicar or priest, a certain monk named Ralph de la Lee, died some time ago; his place is now filled by father Osbert, who says masses and hears confessions in the church. Another person of importance in the place is the lady prioress, Sister Matildis. Of the two, Sister Matildis is perhaps chief, for she shares with John de Grey the right of presentation ; the living is in the gift of Harewold Priory and so also are those of Stevington and Brayfield.†

---

*Considering the poverty of the country about that time, it is really a mystery how the money was raised for so much costly building. Most of the cathedrals, and nearly all the churches in the country, were either built or rebuilt from the time of Henry the First to that of Edward the 2nd.

†The church of Cold Brayfield, Bucks., was given to the Priory at the time of its foundation, by Robert de Blosseville or Blossomville. In 1496 Brayfield church or chapel was in a

Of those who assemble in the church on Sundays, nobody besides Father Osbert, Sir Ralph, and the lady prioress can either read or write, so occasionally, at Christmas, Easter, and other church festivals, more particularly the priest, tries to reach and impress the people, by means of realistic representations, mystery or miracle plays, as they are called. The lapse of time during service is told by the hour glass, which is set in a bracket that branches off from the pulpit; when it has run down the people prepare to leave, or if the service is not finished, the glass is turned about so that the sand may run on again.‡

The priest, and one or two of the nuns, have manuscript missals or breviaries; from these they sing in a sort of minor unison. The hymns and psalms are in Latin, the tunes Gregorian chants, with a range of from four to six notes, or plain song tunes, subject to no definite law of rhythm. As instrumental accompaniment they have the " trom-

---

ruinous condition, the return made at the visitation respecting it being to the effect that it was so through negligence on the part of the prioress and convent of Harewold. —Harvey's " History of the Willey Hundred."

‡The bracket for the hour-glass is still to be seen fastened to the pulpit of Odell church. It is rather a fine specimen of old time wrought-iron work, of about, I should say, the sixteenth century.

pett " and the " pype " played by two rustics ; there is no conception of harmony, but they try to give a sort of body to the tune by means of a *drone* bass, a bass that is like that of the bagpipe, all one sound. In the metropolitan church of the diocese, the cathedral at Lincoln, they have an organ ; it is a clumsy contrivance with large keys four inches square, which they press with the open hand or the fist. The compass of the instrument is about fifteen notes.

These, then, John de Grey, Sister Matildis, Father Osbert, and Ralph Morin, form the political, spiritual and commercial elements of the place ; below these are the common people, the villeins, each holding about thirty acres of land, and the cotters with smaller plots. These holdings are round about the village just outside ; each holding consists approximately of twenty acres of arable land, five acres of meadow land for hay, and five acres of grazing land. The arable land of each estate comprises three large open fields, one of which is fallow. These fields are cut up into long narrow half acre strips. divided by turf balks, and a villein's holding comprehends several strips in each field, the whole of the strips being re-allotted each year by ballot. ach strip has a distinguishing name or mark. The demesne land of the lord consists also of a number of strips distributed about amongst the other strips. This demesne land is cultivated for the lord by those who, being servile tenants, do not pay rent in money nor yet in commodities, such as pepper or wax.

All the more expensive implements of husbandry are owned in common. The ploughing is done by the village ploughs :* for keeping these in order and doing other necessary iron work and repairs, blacksmith Faber is allowed to hold his land free, or partly free of the customary services and dues to the lord ; the same is the case with the village carpenter. The plough is a rude clumsy implement, requiring eight bullocks to draw it ; as each villein is expected to have only two bullocks, they have to co-operate.†

---

*There was usually one plough to from sixty to a hundred and twenty acres. In the Harrold churchwardens' account book I find this entry " Cit Crouch for mending town plough 3s. 3d." From this it appears that there was a plough for common use in the village a little more than a century ago. In the same book are two or three entries of sums paid "for holding town meeting." One wonders whether these " town meetings" were survivals of the old hundred moots, or magistrates meetings, survivals of the old manor court meetings.

†At Pavenham they still show the share and coulter of the old parish plough ; they are kept in a chamber over the porch of the church. This chamber, according to tradition, was the cell of an

When the seed is sown, temporary fences are placed around the fields, but after harvest these are removed, and until next sowing time the cattle and sheep range all over the fields.   The arable and meadow land, on the outskirts of the village, is, in all, about 850 acres. Beyond, like a wide irregular fringe, is the waste or common land, which any villein or cotter in the village has a right to turn his cow or geese upon at any time.   On the river side of the village the common extends, till it meets and mingles with the common lands of similar village communities at Odell, Carlton, Chellington, Felmersham and Turvey; on the other side, towards north and west, the waste prevails till it enters into and is lost in the primeval forest, the inner recesses of which are rarely trodden by human foot.

Of absolute ownership in land nobody has any conception, not even the lord; the right to the land is the right to the use of the land.   The term manor

---

anchorite, an anchorite it would seem of more artistic tastes than the generality of his kind, for some fresco painting is faintly discernible upon the walls.   The ploughshare weighs, I should say, at least fourteen pounds, and the plough it belonged to is said to have required sixteen oxen to draw it.   In these days of match ploughing this saying seems hard to receive, but in olden time it was not at all unusual for twelve oxen to be yoked to a single plough.

means a more or less definite estate of land, and the whole group or body of tenants, who plough and reap thereon in common, of which body the lord is actually or theoretically the head. Hence it follows that the villagers proper are all part and parcel of their respective manors. Robert le Poter cannot leave and go anywhere else without Ralph Morin's consent (as a fact he has no idea of going anywhere else) ; Ralph Morin cannot give him " the sack " so long as he performs the particular duties of his tenure. If, however, through illness or any other cause he shall become incapacitated from performing his allotted tasks, Robert may be transferred, in other words sold. Such sales though, now, are opposed to both custom and sentiment, and are nothing like so common as they were in Saxon times.*

---

*Mr. Gomme maintains that " the tenants of manors were originally no serfs under a lord, but co-equal partners in a social group, to which the lord himself belonged," and that the village community, in Saxon times, was composed of integral units, more or less related members of a little commonwealth, originally a family, who worked very much in common, and held their meetings in the open air, each member having an equal voice and vote in the deliberations. The instances he adduces seem to show conclusively that the constitution of the manor, and manorial jurisdiction, were, in some cases, more democratic, less despotic, or paternal, than appears from Mr. Seebohm's showing. On the whole, though, Mr. Seebohm's seems to be the more *generally* correct view. In Harrold, it is true, at the

The cottages and huts, called messuages, stand in irregular clusters, a little distance from the respective manor houses, or in narrow lanes and pudding-bag yards, to right and left of the main street, along which go the sheep and cattle, and the lumbering carts drawn by oxen. The cottages are all of one story, nearly all of one room. No matter how large the family, father, mother, sons, daughters, often sons-in-law, and daughters-in-law—all live, eat, and sleep in the one apartment, which also has to serve as a shelter for the younger and more delicate of the animal belongings, the calves and lambs, and as a store-room for most of their winter possessions. The furniture consists of a bench or two, wooden bowls, pots and pans. All the family eat from the same dish ; each one has a horn spoon, which, when he has had his meal, he puts in his pocket, or lets hang by a string from his waistband.

---

time we are just now considering, there was no lord of the manor properly speaking, but that proves nothing, only that the old order was changing. Ralph Morin, Richard de Pabenham, and the rest all held their lands "" of said John of said honor." As to Saxon times, three thanes, we read, of King Edward (the Confessor) held the manor, but then they evidently were not fraternal members of a commonwealth, but petty lords, since, according to *Domesday*, they could sell it (the manor) to whom they would.

The clothing of the men is of home-spun wool, and a sort of tunic, made of the tanned skin of the sheep, or some other animal, with more or less of the wool or hair on; it slips over the head, reaches down nearly to the knees, and is drawn around the waist by a belt, with a brass buckle. The feet, usually, are encased in " clouted shoon," but the legs are bare, or else plaited around with thin strips of leather; the ordinary head covering is the thick matted hair.

In the main or High-street, which is rather a tortuous drive than a street, are two or three tenements, rather better than the cottages of the villeins, but there are no shops. The various members of each family have to co-operate, and so are their own bakers, butchers, wool - workers, clothiers, and leather dressers. Now and then there is a little bartering one with another; if William Romay wants more cheese than he has, he gets it from Robert le Champiun, in exchange for some pork or beans. The original Sanders's shop is not opened, mainly because groceries are as yet unknown. The few candles they need they make by dipping dried rushes into melted fat, until they become about as thick as the little finger; these give just the suitable glimmer

for them to tell their cheerful evening tales by—of
the sports of the fairies, the tricks of witches, and
the antics of goblins. In winter, though, there is
really nothing to sit up for. Soon after seven they
all settle down for the long night's repose, and
silence reigns undisturbed, save for the baying of
dogs, or the more distant howling of wolves.

But, though, as regards the necessaries of life,
the village is self-dependent, an oasis separated from
all the rest of the world, there are two or three
articles, salt for instance, and iron for the blacksmith's use, that they are bound to get somehow
from outside. And besides these, which are native
productions, there is a limited demand for a few
other things that are made or grown only in foreign
countries. The silk, worn on special occasions by
Lady Morin, was not produced in England, nor the
spectacles used by the old lady, her mother. For the
supply of articles such as these they are indebted to
Venetian and Florentine mariners and merchants
who to English ports bring argosies of all manner
of precious things, silks and carpets from Turkey and
Persia, dyes, ivory, brass, sulphur, glass, spectacles,
mirrors, paper, spices. From the ports these wares
are conveyed to the various great fairs, held at differ-

ent times at Nottingham, Cambridge, Leicester, St. Ives, and other towns. These fairs last for several days, or even a fortnight,* booths are erected in the streets, and people from all round resort to them for the finery and ornaments, which are to make them the observed of all observers in their little community.

The bulk, however, of the wares are taken up the river highways, or get distributed by chapmen, who, moving along the great Roman roads, branch off here and there as they reach the tracks leading to the various villages, where they sell their goods to the few who have money to buy, or else barter them for wool, skins, and other village products. In such way Robert le Champiun and Richard de Esseby obtain the pepper and cumin that they pay as rent to their respective landlords, Richard de Pabenham and John de Grey.

The population of the village is about two hundred. During the last fifty years it has increased a little, else it has been nearly stationary for centuries. No need to look out new lands for surplus human beings; war famine and pestilence act as unfailing "checks." Every male in the village, between sixteen and sixty,

---

*The Stourbridge fair used to last three weeks.

is liable to be called on to help make up the contingent, which Sir John is required to equip, and himself lead forth if need be for the service of the king. Then the cottages are mere hovels, without chimneys, stairs, or windows; there are no sanitary arrangements or conveniences whatever, and so every few years plague or some other epidemic disease comes and takes off one in ten of the people. Verily, it is a time of selection, weeding and survival. You and I, friend, are here, because our forefathers and foremothers happened to be a bit tougher than some of their neighbours.

This is one view of the good old times, yet let us not finish off our picture in such gloomy colours. Life, usually, has its compensations. Being shut off, comparatively, from the outside world, the people feel somewhat as members of one great family. They bear each others burdens, and so escape many of the worries and anxieties inevitable to a freer individual existence.

And of this family the lord is more than a figure head. The roads mostly are bad, travelling toilsome and dangerous, so Sir Ralph, save on rare occasions, stays at home among his own people; he knows every man in the village, and when he meets them salutes them with: "Well, Thomas"; "How are you, Roger?"; "Good morning, Robert, I want you to come to the manor to-morrow, or the next day, to finish threshing that barley. You have only been one day, I think, this week." Her ladyship, too, knows the women and most of the children, and keeps goose-grease and herbs always ready for sending out.

They have their active joys, too, in their rough way. There are plenty of holidays, Plough Monday, Distaff Day, Candlemas, Collop Monday, Shrove Tuesday, and several more. At these times, and on Sunday afternoons, after morning service, the people assemble on the green or the common outside, and play at quoits or football, the priest often joining in their diversions; then, as the games proceed, and they get excited, they shout and hustle, and play the fool, as youths are apt to do in more modern times.

But the favourite and most dignified sport is archery. Every village has its crack shots, with either the long or the cross bow, and on May-Day the archers, from several villages round, meet at some suitable spot, such as the slope below Chellington Church, to contend for the championship. To these contests come not only Sir Ralph and his family, but the Wahulls,* also the lords of Odell, and the Pabenhams, from Pavenham. It is thought well to encourage this sport, for archers are indispensable in warfare, and English archers are renowned for their strength and skill. The crowning feat is, at a distance of fifty paces, to split a willow wand in two.

After the shooting there are games, some of them mere foolery, making ugly faces through a horse's collar, and the like ; then there is quarter staff, and morris dancing, and then a medley dance, or rather a jig, in which all join, all sorts and conditions, to general accompaniment of shouting and laughter:

> Now is the month of Maying,
> When merry lads are playing,
> > Fal lal lal la la ;
> Each with his bonny lass,
> A-dancing on the grass,
> > Fal lal lal la la.

Before we proceed on our way it will perhaps be worth while to go back a few pages, and read over again the names of the villagers. As Bedfordshire

---

*On the 30th November, 1346, Sir John de Woodhul, or Wahull, had summons to be at Sandwich, on Monday after the feast of St. Lucy, the Virgin, with his family, and what men he could raise, properly armed with arrows, to attend the king to France.

was in the Danelagh, I thought it was probable that
some of the names might be Danish, so I sent the
list of them to Mr. W. G. Collingwood, M.A., of
Coniston. In reply, he says: "There is very little
of Danish, evidently, in Harewold; Esseby and
Montibz are places in Scandinavian districts, from
which the families have come. Ketel, too, seems to
be Scandinavian. It strikes me, as interesting, that
none of the christian names are of an early and Saxon
or Danish type; they are all Norman-English, and so
are most of the surnames chiefly from places. Howel
means a Welshman."

People, by this time, had evidently begun to emi-
grate from village to village, and good families had
begun to come down in the world. I suppose it always
was full of ups and downs. And yet, I do not believe
the lot of a "serf" was so bad; he had what we all
want and can not get—fixity of tenure. He had to pay
a "fine" when he married his daughter, and so on,
but he knew what his liabilities were, and he was not
subject to fluctuations of market and foreign competition. Compared with the struggle for life of the
present day he had "much to be thankful for."

As illustrating this "coming down" of good
families it may be noted that one of the free tenants

of Ralph Morin bore the same Norman surname.
We are not to conclude though, I suppose, that all
bearing Norman names descended from ancestors of
high degree.   No doubt many came in the wake of
the Conqueror simply as emigrants, just as, after the
inundation in Flanders, Flemish weavers came over,
hoping to find a protectress in the Queen, Matilda,
the wife of the Conqueror, who herself was a native
of Flanders.   Amongst these Harewold tenants it
will be remembered that there was a William le
Flemyng.   Flaundrine Manduyt, too, the benefactor
of the Knights Templars, was, no doubt, a Fleming.

Several villeins, it would seem, had no proper surnames, but were known as merely the sons or
daughters of their parents.   Thus we have Reginald,
son of Reginald; Gilbert, son of Matthew; Isabel,
daughter of Galf (Galfrid); and several others.

About this time, in the year 1399, it is recorded
that the river suddenly changed its course and left a
dry channel for three miles between Snelson and
Harrold.*   Now the Hoang Ho, a rapid, turbulent,

---

*In the yere of our redemption 1399 the first of January and
22 of King R.2 in this countie nere to the towne of Harwood
the River Ouse suddenly stayd her course and divided it selfe
soe that for the space of 3 miles the wonted chanell thereof laye
drye to the great amazement of the beholders and ever since

Chinese river, often indulges in these destructive pranks, but I own I was rather surprised when I read such a rowdy report of so sober and generally well-conducted a river as the Ouse, whose very name is suggestive of quiet and decorum. According to the evidence of geology it has been wild and wanton enough formerly, in its young days, but we charitably hoped that it had sown its wild oats and settled down thousands of years ago.

Then, there is a tradition that the river once stood still, tired no doubt ; you see it had been running a long while, so it stood still, rested for the space of three hours. Even this is not so wonderful as what is happening every day close by. At Maulden, they tell me that, for some distance, a stream there runs up hill. That beats our river Ouse altogether. We have not many hills hereabouts, but, where there are any, we have to own that our river has rather a sneaking way of avoiding and slipping past them ; it does not face and surmount them like that brave little stream at Maulden.

---

observed as a prodigious token or foreshowing of that great and lamentable division in the kingdom betwixt the families of York and Lancaster which the next yeare followed and continewed the tyme of 90 whole yeres together with blodshed and losse — Note to Map of Bedfordshire 1610.

F

THE REFORMATION PERIOD.

INTERIOR OF YE NUNNE'S HALL, HAREWOLD.

From FISHER'S "Sketches of Bedfordshire."

The Reformation Period.

THE priory, as I have said, stood on Mow Hills, not far from the river. Walking over the hummocky ground it looks as though the place must have been blasted by a curse, for verily not one stone is left upon another; you cannot even trace the plan of the building. Going towards the old ash tree you make out what looks like an ancient pathway or the grass-covered foundations of a wall. Elsewhere all is confusion. It was not a large place, nor yet wealthy, like some of the priories—Elstow for instance. The nett yearly income of Elstow Abbey was £256, derived from ninety-four properties, bequeathed at various times and in different parts of the country; that of Harewold was £40 18s. 2d. This looks very small, only we have to take into account the difference in the relative values of money, then and now. The pay of a labourer about that time for mowing grass was a penny a day, or by the " gret " fivepence an acre; from this and other data we gather that a penny represented at least a shilling of our present money, and so this £40 18s. 2d. was equivalent to about £500 a year now,* not a very large sum, yet amply sufficient, one would think, for four or five nuns with their presumably simple wants.

The income of the priory was derived mainly from property in Kent, but, as time went on, other small properties were bequeathed to it, a plot of land at Sharnbrook, a messuage and land at Stevington, Felmersham, Hinwick, Biddenham, Bromham, Bletsoe, Turvey, Stagsden, Carlton, and other places round about. In those days hell was a vivid reality and people had a great idea of securing the intercession of the so-called religious, and the way to secure this intercession was to give either money or property to a monastery or nunnery.

The priory was in existence for nearly 400 years, from A.D. 1150 till 1536. For nearly 400 years a succession of Sisters abode here, nursing, busying themselves with embroidery, perhaps, or weaving, doing no doubt some good in the village, but

---

*Cobbett gives the income at £47 3s. 2d., equivalent, according to his mode of calculation, to £943 3s. 4d., a penny in the 15th century having, he maintains, the same purchasing power or value as twenty pence at the time he wrote, in 1829.

engaged mostly in living what was called the religious life, going through a course of observances and austerities which could be of no earthly use or benefit to any living being.* When I walk slowly over Mow Hills and think of the long procession of Sisters who, one little group after another, lived here their day and passed away, I confess I am not conscious of that sense of awe and reverence which one feels or ought to feel when treading ground made sacred by the feet of the departed good and great.

To my mind monasticism, whatever else it may have been, was a cover and excuse for a vast amount of unsuspected laziness. In the world there are always a number of people, unfortunately a large number, who do not like work and will put up with a good deal if they can in some way avoid having to earn their own living. It is absurd and an evasion to talk about retiring from the world ; all the work of the world is in the world, and those who, under any pretext, decline to engage in work of some serviceable kind are parasites living upon the labour of others.

---

*All the lady prioresses seem to have had euphonious names. The first was named Juliana, the second Basilia, then follow Agnes, Matildis, Cecilia, and so on. Beyond their names, however, they have left no record.

For the world is not primarily either a church or a drawing room. No, primarily it is a workshop and the first duty of every person is to see to it that he earns the share that he necessarily consumes of the common store. There is no escape from the dilemma; we are all consumers and we either fairly earn our keep or in some more or less clandestine way we steal it. "I pray not that thou wouldst take them out of the world but that thou wouldst keep them from the evil." Here is doctrine healthier, manlier, than is to be found in the rules for saint-making of Saint Benedict, Saint Ignatus, or saint anybody else.

And the evils of the monastic system were not merely negative. Satan finds some mischief still for idle hands to do. In 1530 Longland, Bishop of Lincoln, wrote a long letter of remonstrance to the Abbess of Elstow, because the nuns kept almost open house for men, women, and children, "and many other inconvenyents hath thereby ensewed." Dr. Layton, one of the commissioners appointed by Henry the Eighth to enquire into the conduct of the religious houses, in his letter to Lord Cromwell, makes against the nuns of Harwold, a yet more direct

charge.* Soon after, in 1536, Sister Elinor, the last
of the lady prioresses, was called on to surrender the
keys of the priory, the nuns were dismissed, and
their lands given to others.†

Henry's method was rough but it was effective. Before the dissolution there were 2319 monasteries and
nunneries in the country; if they had been dealt
with by ordinary process of law, hundreds of these
might have persisted down to this day.

---

*Another priorie, called Harwoulde, wherein was iiij or v
nunnes with the prioress; one of them hade two faire chyldren
another one and no mo. My lorde Mordant (of Turvey)
dwelling nygh the saide howse intyssed the young nunnes to
breke up the cofer whereas the covent seale was: Sir John
Mordant, his eldyste son then present ther perswading them to
the same causede ther the prioress and hir folysshe yong floke
to seale a writying in Latten; what therein is conteynede nother
the priores nor hir sisters can telle, saying that my Lord Mordant
tellith them that hit ys but a leasse of a benifice improperite
with other tenenderyse.—*Dr. Layton to Cromwell, Dec.* 22,
1535. "Suppression cf Monasteries," Camden Remains.

†The site of the Priory building, and the adjoining land, have
descended to the Dowager Countess Cowper. The Priory
farm, with part of Nun Woods, is the property of Mrs.
Gambier.—Harvey's "History of the Willey Hundred."

Since writing the above, owing to the death of Mrs. Gambier,
the property has been offered for sale. The farm is now tenanted
by Mr. G. Preston. Near the farm house is a dish-shaped
depression, called "Bottom bottoms" which, evidently at one

The pope excommunicated Henry, Henry excommunicated the pope, and the question now remained who was to be head of the church in England. The king answered this in characteristic fashion. He would be head of the church. This was a shock to not only devout Catholics, but also to the more thorough of the Protestants—the Puritans who would have neither pope nor king, nor any other earthly person as their spiritual head. The clergymen, who objected whether as Puritans or Papists to the supremacy of the king, were called recusants, and of these was Marmaduke Pullen, in 1577 vicar or curate of Harrold. Other recusants in this neighbourhood were W. Ralph, of Stevington, Richard Dove, of Bletsoe, and Ralph Jones, of St. Cuthberts, Bedford.

Twenty years after Pullen was suspended, Robert Paull became vicar here, and he, as soon as he got settled, began to keep a parish register. It is written at first in Early English, and so is not easy now to make out. The heading of this register reads " Christenings, mariages, and burials from ye feast of St. Michael the Archangel, 1598, until the annun-

---

time, served for a fish pond. Nun's Wood, as it is still called, covered formerly an area of 120 acres, but half of it of late years has been cleared. The trees are nearly all oaks.

ciation of St. Mary, the Virgin, 1599." The first
entry is appropriately a baptism. "The 21st Nov.,
Johan, ye daughter of Wm. Cleton, was baptised."

It is not unlikely that the Harrold Claysons are
descended from the family this little maid belonged
to, the name, getting modified afterwards as frequently happened, or they may have sprung from the
Caysons, who, in the time of Charles the First, lived
at Dungee. According to a certificate later on, I find
that Zaccheus Clayson, a stonemason, came here in
1779 from Brayfield on the Green; but we know
there were Claysons here long before them. On the
very first pages of the oldest churchwardens' book we
meet with the names of Uriah and William Clayson.

One of the earliest names in this register is Ffary,
spelt at different periods in half a dozen different
ways. At one time the family was related, in name
at least, to those sprightly little beings who used to
dance in the meadows by moonlight and recline
when they were tired on toadstools. Steam and
science since then have annihilated them unfortunately. The loss, however, is not altogether
unmitigated. As we all have read, they were guilty
of the reprehensible trick of changing peoples' babies,

which, to mothers, of course, was very annoying and perplexing.

Robinson meant originally Robin's son and seems always to have been spelt in the same way, and so was Pettit and Neal and Knight. Franklin, another old Harrold name, meant originally a freeholder, one who held his land free of the customary service and dues to the lord. These franklins or freeholders were mostly of Danish extraction. There is one peculiarity about this family; Robert seems always to have been a favourite Christian name with them down to the present day.

Of surnames derived from occupations we have besides Franklin, Fuller, Fisher, Brewer, Butcher, Baker, Glover, Potter, Smith, Sadler, Sawyer, Tailor. Woodmancey. More numerous still are the surnames derived from places round about—Bletsoe, Bedford, Clapham, Campton, Charlton, Harrold, Hoton, Hardwick, Ireland, Islop, Layton, Odell, Potton, Stoughton, Woolston, Wolverton, Wootton, Yardley. Of names of places more distant we find Boston, Bosworth, Dudley, Selby, and others. These names no doubt got started in some such way as this. Tom Somebody came, say, from Bletsoe. The people around knew not his surname, perhaps he hardly knew it himself, so they called him Bletsoe Tom, and afterwards Tom Bletsoe.

From these registers I have culled a good many more names, and I should like, did time permit, to pause longer over them, but before we pass on let me say a word or two about Christian names. Women's Christian names in the time of Elizabeth were very beautiful and musical. Elizabeth is the most general and that is not very beautiful, but it was the name of the queen, and it shews a little how immensely popular she was when we find that a century after her death Elizabeth was still one of the most popular names. Taking the first twenty-four years of this register, the names in the order of their frequency run thus: Elizabeth, Joan, Anne, Alice, Agnes, Mary, Margaret, Susanna, Margery, Helen, Martha, Lettice, Sarah, Katherine, Dorothy.

The men's names, as you might expect, are not nearly so pretty. I give them also in the order of their frequency—Thomas, William, John, Robert, Richard, George, Nicholas, Anthony, Henry, Edward. Comparing these two lists, you will notice that, with the exception of two, all the commonest men's names are common names still. That is to say, there has been no general change. Women's names, on the other hand, are constantly changing. Fifty years ago Emma, Jane, Eliza, Sarah, Susan, Hannah, Caroline, were among the most common names; now these are all discarded, and if you consult a school register of to-day you will find that the prevailing girls' names now are Ethel, Edith, Hilda, Florence, Gertrude. These, in turn, will shortly disappear, and give place to others which are already being evolved in novels.

This comparative fixity of men's names is due, in part, to the natural desire of parents that the son should inherit the father's name as well as his property; but, apart from this, which affects only one son here and there in a family, men seem in this, as in most other respects, less eager for change, less versatile and vivacious than women. Take dress in illustration. What style of head-gear do women stick to with half the persistence that we do to the chimney-pot hat? The coal-scuttle bonnet, the Devonshire hat, the Dolly Varden, the plate, the pork pie, the Covent Garden! All are creatures of a day in comparison with the hat we men wear on Sundays. We ring a round of changes upon it, it is true, we narrow the brim, then we widen it, then we curl up the side, we lower the dome to six inches, anon we exalt it to twelve, but through all mutations it remains fundamentally the same, the dear old chimney-pot. "Time cannot wither, nor custom stale its infinite variety."

I referred just now to some of the older names in the register; others there are nearly—perhaps—quite as ancient: Pratt, Allen, Osborn, Bailey, Goff, Christopher, Crouch—Cit Crouch, as he was usually called, the Vulcan of his day, the father of a line of Crouches, the Tubal Cains of the village.

But though there are family trees in Harrold, which got planted here hundreds of years ago, no one tree has ever spread half over the place; there seems always to have been considerable diversity of population. In many villages certain families predominate like clans; in one there is a tribe of Crawleys, in another of Garners. Some years ago I ran my eye over the voters' list, which was tacked on to the church door of a neighbouring village; there were 74 voters, and of these 17 or nearly 24 per cent. were named Hulett. There is not, and, so far as one can ascertain, there never has been, anything corresponding to this in Harrold.

Yet another lesson from these names.   It is pretty
generally known that the lace industry was introduced
into this county by French Huguenots, who, to escape
the persecution they were exposed to in their own
country, came over here, bringing their lace pillows
with them.   Cranfield is named as the village that
received them, but it appears from the occurrence of
French names in this register, that some of them
must have settled in Harrold.   The names France
and French, we may suppose, originated in the same
way as the local surnames I have just referred to ; but,
besides these, in the earlier pages of the register, we
find such native French names as Orpin, Paton, and
Peignolles.

Confirmation of this assumed Huguenot immi-
gration is furnished by a coin found on another
part of Mr. Pickering's farm.   It is a fine silver coin
of Henry the Fourth of France, and bears the legend
Henricus iv. Gallae et Navarrae Rex.   This is the
King whose equestrian statue adorns the famous Pont
Neuf in Paris.   Henry was, at one time, the champion
of French Protestantism, the " Henry of Navarre,"
in Macaulay's stirring *Song of the Huguenots.*

" ' The king is come to marshal us, in all his armour drest,
    And he has bound a snow white plume upon his gallant crest.
    He looked upon his people, and a tear was in his eye,

He looked upon the traitors and his glance was stern and
    high :
Right graciously he smiled on us, as rolled from wing to
    wing,
Down all our line a deafening shout, 'God save our Lord,
    the King '
And if our standard bearer fall, as fall full well he may,
For never saw. I promise, yet, of such a bloody fray.
Press where ye see my white plume shine, amidst the ranks
    of war,
And be your oriflamme to-day, the helmet of Navarre.' "

I have, somehow, formed a high opinion of the
vicar who began the register, the Rev. Robert Paull.
By his work I seem to know him, a cultured modest
man, orderly in his life, painstaking, and con-
scientious in the discharge of his duties. None of
the later registers were kept like his. Everything,
about it was first well thought over, then honestly
done. In size it is about one third wider than deep,
the parchment of excellent quality, untearable, yet
soft and flexible ; it is a pleasure to turn over the
leaves. I find that at one time you had a parchment
maker, or makers, here ; so let us hope the parchment
for your register was made in Harrold.

Then the ink ! We have no better even now.
The letters look as fresh as if they had been written
only a year or two ago. One wonders, too, how,
with a quill pen, he managed to write such fine

graceful lines. The new—that is our style of writing, was coming in then, but he preferred to keep to the old, which, if it took longer, was unquestionably more picturesque, and at that time more perusable by ordinary people.

There is just one entry which seems to show that our excellent vicar was not wanting in humour. In the year 1600 there were fifteen births and nine deaths, but no marriages, and so in the marriage column he wrote the simple words, "Nulla Nuptia." "No marriage."

"Nulla Nuptia!" "Nulla Nuptia!" How sad and mournful is the sound. It is like the refrain of Poe's bird of ill omen; croaked the raven, "Nevermore"; quoth the parson, "Nulla Nuptia." "Nulla Nuptia." It only occurs this once, yet how across the centuries does it echo back, as a reproach to the young men of that generation. Just imagine ourselves, the largest half of us opening our weekly paper every Saturday for a whole year, and finding no matrimonial fixtures or announcements; no wedding presents; no trousseaux; no bridesmaids; no anything! We live in far different times now. As you take, like Isaac, your meditative evening walk, what time the young folk in pairs go forth; as you see them moving pensively beside the hedgerows, saying little and heeding not the passers by at all, you regard the sight, the most blissful (so Burns assures us), in this weary mortal round, you regard the sight, I say, as a sign, a pledge. a sort of rainbow assurance, that such a calamity, as is implied in this Nulla Nuptia, is not likely to occur in Harrold again, at any rate not in your time.

From this register, too, we can find out very nearly how large was the village, what was the population, in the time of Elizabeth. The number of births, taking twenty-four years, was on an average about thirteen ; the deaths nine. The births now average twenty-four, the deaths fifteen. As the population, now, is nearly 1000,* it must then have been about 550. The population of Bedford, in the time of Elizabeth, was about 1200, only a little more than twice that of Harrold.

The wage of labourers was sixpence to sevenpence a day ; carpenters a shilling. Wheat averaged 30s.,

---

*In 1801 the population was about 780, in 1831—970, in 1861 —1116. Since then agricultural depression has operated as it has done in most of the villages, though the introduction of the leather trade has served to some extent as a check or restorative. The population at the last census was 976.

barley 15s. The highest price for an ox was £5 :
average price of a sheep 7s. 9d. There was keen
interest in life just then and much gaiety. America
was newly discovered, and travellers' tales were
everywhere rehearsed and discussed. Tobacco and the
potato were coming into use. Bacon was thinking
out his philosophy ; Shakespeare, then a young man,
was bringing out his play. With the people there
was no lack of holidays; on these occasions, and
sometimes on Sundays the lords of misrule, the mad-
caps of the village, went capering about, decked with
garlands and ribbons, their legs gartered with bells,
riding hobby horses and dragons.   In this array they
would prance up Church Lane, through the church-
yard, and right into the church, so that the congregation mounted on the pews to see them.*

*Social *England* --Vol. 3

THE COMMONWEALTH AND AFTER.

The Commonwealth and After.

LET us now move on a few years down to the time
of the Stuarts, and the Commonwealth. The
Orlebars, now, are living at the hall, one of them,
Richard Orlebar, being constable of Harrold; to him as
constable of the Willey Hundred Sir Samuel Luke,
one of the most active supporters of the Parliament,
addressed a number of interesting letters, the
originals of which are still in the possession of the
Orlebar family at Hinwick. The purport of these
letters we shall better understand if we consider for a
few minutes the circumstances which occasioned
them.

Archbishop Laud, with the approval of the king,
was about this time making great efforts to secure
uniformity of public worship, but he met here with
much resistance. "My visitors," he reports to the
king, "found Bedfordshire the most tainted of any
part of the diocese, and, in particular, Mr. Bulkeley
is sent to the High Commission for Nonconformity."

This Peter Bulkeley succeeded his father, Dr. Bulkeley, as rector of Odell, in 1620. His sister was the wife of Sir Oliver St. John, of Keysoe, and mother of the Oliver St. John who afterwards became Lord Chief Justice to Cromwell. Cromwell's mother was a St. John, consequently Peter Bulkeley was distantly related to both Cromwell and Hampden. "Bulkeley was," says Dr. Brown, "a learned man, highly esteemed by his parishioners, and all who knew him, but, finding he could not with a good conscience retain his ministry, he took sorrowful leave of his good people of Odell, and, accompanied by Zachary Symmes, of the Priory Church at Dunstable, sailed for New England, where he joined the Pilgrim Fathers in 1635. Subsequently, he pursued his way through "unknowne woods" to the banks of the Musketaquid River, where he founded the city of Concord, the first inland plantation of the Massachusetts Colony."

Peter Bulkeley's grand-daughter was married in 1665 to the Rev. John Emerson. From this union sprang Ralph Waldo Emerson. And thou, Odell, art not the least among the villages of Bedfordshire, for out of thee went forth one who became ancestor to the famous American thinker and writer.

In 1636, Laud again reported to the king that in Bedfordshire there was great opposition to the erection of altar rails, and to the kneeling before them. Previous to this, from the time of the Reformation and the abolition of the mass, there had been no rails round the communion table.* By a compromise, arrived at in the time of Elizabeth, it was decided, after much controversy, that the table was to stand in the church, where the altar used to stand before the Reformation, *except at the Celebration*, when it had to be placed where the congregation could most conveniently see and hear the minister. When the communion service was over it was to be returned to its former place. In opposition to this practice Laud sought to set up, in all churches, fixed altars, with altar rails, to which the people were to go and kneel. According to a petition of George Daniell, vicar of Steventon, although the people preferred the order of administration they had been accustomed to, Laud's " Commissarie " at the Court of Bedford, "ordered steppes to be raised at the upper end of the chancel of St. Paul's in Bedford, and gave strict orders that the communion table be sette there north and south." He afterwards

---

* " John Bunyan," by Dr. Brown.—p. 9-16.—*Isbister.*

reprimanded the vicar, John Bradshaw, because he did not keep within the rails, but came down to the communicants, and he further "gave orders to the communicants to come up to the rails about the communion table, and first went up thither himself to show them how."

Another grievance of George Daniell's was that in apportioning the tax imposed upon the clergy for the king's expedition to Scotland, the commissary demanded from Daniell £5 instead of forty six shillings; and from Thomas Wells, the rector of Carlton £6. "This was greatly too much, and, because he did not pay, he cited Mr. Wells (though a hundred years olde) and because he did not appear he suspended him, and called him an old owle." Truly there are strange contradictions in human nature. This is he who instructed the communicants at St. Paul's, Bedford, in the way they ought to receive the sacrament.

Proceedings such as these were not likely to win over the common people in the county to the Royalist side. Most of the leading families already inclined the other way. The St. Johns, of Bletsoe, as I said just now, were related to Cromwell and Hampden, and naturally shared their views. Oliver St. John was counsel for Hampden, in his famous contest with the king about ship money. In the Long Parliament, Bedfordshire was represented by four staunch Parliamentarians :—Sir Beauchamp, St. John, of Bletsoe, Sir Oliver Luke, of Cople Wood End, his son Sir Samuel Luke, and Sir John Burgoyne. Scarcely a family, says Mr. Harvey, could the king count on in Bedfordshire only the Dyves of Bromham ; of these the most active and influential was Sir Lewis Dyve, and he, in July 1642, " had to flee for his life and swam across the river where it flows past Bromham Hall."

The drift of opinion in Bedfordshire was shown yet more unmistakably on the 16th of March, 1641, when a petition was presented to parliament by Sir John Burgoyne, accompanied by some two thousand persons, " the high sheriff, knights, gentlemen, ministers, freeholders and others, inhabitants of the county of Bedford." The Parliament were much gratified with this demonstration ; it was such a strengthening of their hands, for the processionists rode through the city four abreast, on their way to Westminster. I, myself, says a contemporary, " did see above two thousand of these men come riding from Finsbury Fields, four in a rank, with their protestations in their hats."

These two thousand Bedfordshire men, no doubt, meant, by their demonstration, to strengthen the hands of the Parliament; still their action was altogether peaceable and constitutional; it was the unconstitutional attempt of the king to gain his ends by force, that brought the representatives of the people to see that they must take up an attitude of defence, and that no time was to be lost. On the fourth of January, 1642, the king sought to arrest the five members; on the twenty-second of the same month the following letter was written :—

" To Ye Constables of Harrold,—I have received and other letter from Sr Samuell Luke, Knight, wherein you are desired to give notice to some of your chiefe inhabitants of your p^{r}ish y^t they in — — — doe bring ye numbers and names of all those who are to serve as dragoons and foote soldiers for defence of his Maties person* ye parliament and kingdom and ye same to deliver unto Willm Haston Gent at ye Redd Lyon in Bedd on Tuesday next wch will be taken as an acceptable service. — Dated 22th of January 1642.—Ro. TAPP."

---

*Down to the appointment of Cromwell to the chief command the parliament in their addresses and declarations always used this form.

This letter, it would appear, got no answer. Meanwhile both parties were preparing for the inevitable struggle. In August the Royal Standard was raised at Nottingham, the king having appealed to his loyal supporters everywhere to bring him money, horses, and arms, on the security of his forests and parks, for repayment of the principal, and eight per cent. interest. The Parliament, on their side, offered the same rate of interest to all who should bring in money or plate, or furnish men or arms; they also issued a pamphlet called a "*Declaration of the Lords and Commons assembled in Parliament, concerning his Majesties advancing with his army towards London, with direction that all the trained bands and volunteers be put into a readinesse.*" A copy of this pamphlet is preserved among the Orlebar papers. After describing the unfortunate condition of the kingdom, through the rapacity of his Majesty's soldiers, it goes on to say, "By these violences and oppressions they have so exhausted those parts (Shropshire) that his Majesty cannot stay long about Shrewsbury, and it is the earnest desire of the cavaliers that he would march forward towards London, those rich and fruitful countries in the way being likely to yield them a full supply of their

necessities, and the wealth of London a full satis-
faction of their hope." They, therefore, advise and
decree, " that the counties through which the king's
army is to pass, doe associate themselves, and draw
all their forces together for the mutual defence of
their persons and goods from oppression and
spoile."

This pamphlet is dated *Sabati*, 15 Octob., 1642.
A few days later the following letter was written:—

"To ye Constables of Harrold. By order of a
warrant from Sir Thomas Alston, Knight, Sir
Beauchamp St. John, Knight, and Thomas Rolt,
Esq.,* doe require you to warne and enjoine
all ye trainord Souldiers and supplies within your
P^{ish}, that they appear at Bedd in their arms
compleat on Saturday next by 8 of ye clock in ye
morning, there to be trained and exercised, and to
receive such further instructions and directions as
there and then shall be enjoyned them as you will
answer ye contempt thereof and hereof faile you
not.—Dated 20th of October, 1642.—ROBT. TAPP."

From this it appears that Sir Samuel Luke and
other county notabilities were at this time at

*Of Milton Ernest.

Bedford, getting together the levies from the various hundreds in the county, to swell the army of Essex, who was moving towards Oxford with orders from Parliament, "to pursue the king and by battle or other ways to rescue him from his perfidious counsellors and restore him to Parliament."

Money was wanted also as well as men. Parliament had made a call upon the country for £400,000. The quota of which sum to be raised in the Willey Hundred was £227 19s. 0d., and Sir Samuel Luke and his associates, it would seem, had not only to get the men but to get the money too. In imagination we see them of an evening gathered around the spacious hearth, with its log fire, in the large room of "Ye Redd Lyon" talking over the events of the day, or at the oak table, with a map spread out before them, planning their part of the campaign, and discussing the general prospects of the war. Whilst thus sitting in council a report reaches them that the rector of St. Cuthbert's, a certain Giles Thorne, persists in praying for the king, and from his pulpit defies the authority of Parliament. So one Sunday Lord St. John goes, with a few of his troopers, clattering down to St. Cuthbert's Church, and at the close of the service he arrests the offending parson and marches him off to Sir Samuel Luke.

The Parliamentary army after this moved on to Leighton, and from there another letter was written :—

" Whereas all cannot but be sensible of ye great miseryes and calamities, y^t this kingdom hath a long time groaned under, and is likely, by inevitable necessity, to be totally waisted and consumed by a long and tedious warre, through the desperate malice of our most wicked and blood thirstye enemies, who hunger after the ruin and confusion of us, and all others well affected to ye publicke, having no other end in their counsells and actions but to swallow our estates and the very bread, breath, and livelyhood of us, our parliament, wives, and children, unless some speedy and desperate cure be applyed to ye allmost immedicinable disease. The wise and serious consideration of these things hath caused our parliament, for our present cure, to move a generall riseinge of all well affected persons and counties throughout the kingdom for their present aide and assistance, and of this have given the lord generall information, whose letters and commands are now come to signify his and their pleasure therein."

The letter then goes on to say that they must, without further delay, send on the recruits with provisions and one month's pay; "And hereof fayle not, as you will answere ye contrary at your perills." —Dated this 2nd of June, 1643. To Ye Constables of Harrold.—Ro. Tapp.

Even this vigorous missive seems not to have had the desired effect, so Sir Samuel Luke himself took up his pen, and wrote as follows :—

" Whereas warn^{gs} and let^{res} have issued out into this country to stirre up my country men for a generall riseinge to dispatch this great businesse now in hand but such fruits hath not proceeded from this way as was in so faire a manner and in so great a good desired and expected. Theis are therefore to signify unto you and my desire is it may be published in every parish wthin your Devisions wth all speed that I will noe longer dally wth or by more faire wayes and meanes — — my country men seeinge it is allmost altogethere vaine and fruite lesse but I am resolved y^t if all persons in every parish between 16 and 60 beinge able to carry armes shall not severally and speedily appeare wth all provisions wth them and armes and weapons for ye service of ye state and

H

theire owne safety I will proceede against such cold
insensible persons and parishes of this county with
ye rigor and severity as is done in other places y^t ye
good may not all wayes remayne scoft and derided
at but y^t they shall and may receive such ease and
comfort by such my proceedinge as is agreable to all
manner of equitie and give confidence and y^t let them
know w^t all such as doe come are to march away
presently and therefore desire them to come provided
for ye purpose.—June ye 7, 1643.—To ye high
Constables of ye hundred of Willy and to either of
them this on Saterday, 10 June, 1643."

Altogether over a dozen letters were written, the
originals of which, as I have before said, are in the
possession of Mrs. Orlebar, of Hinwick.   We are not
to conclude, however, that the Constable, Richard
Orlebar, was really hostile to the Parliament ; most
probably, like many others just then, he hardly knew
whom to recognise as the head of the State, and so
thought it safest to remain neutral as long as he
could.   It is said that some of Cromwell's soldiers
afterwards came through Harrold, called at the hall,
and demanded horses of the coachman who happened
to be just then left in charge.   As he resisted, one of
the soldiers struck him with his sword so that he died
soon after.

Such accidents or incidents were bound to occur in civil warfare, and prove nothing either way. The only pronounced Royalist about here, so far as we know, was Sir Henry Cayson, of Dungee Wood. Like so many more he had, after the war, to compound for his offences against the Parliament. Dr. Brown quotes a petition from his son, a youth of seventeen, praying that his father's estate might not be taken away altogether for his delinquency, for that while Sir Henry and his lady had left "his own house in the Parliamentary quarters, and gone to visit his wife's friends in Bristol, while it was the king's garrison, they both dyed there, one shortly after the other, leaving nine children, all infants of tender yeares, fatherlesse and motherlesse."*

It would seem that the sharp and emphatic letter of Sir Samuel Luke compelled the Constable of Harrold at last to call out his recruits. Parliament had constituted Newport a garrison and had ordered that the county of Bedford within fourteen days

---

*The vicar, Thomas Fawcet, also was a Royalist. As he absolutely refused to pay the taxes imposed on him by Parliament during the civil war, his living was sequestrated and he himself twice imprisoned. The king must have found his zeal embarrassing, or at any rate useless, for he indirectly ordered him to comply, saying to Col. Fawcet "Why should your brother ruin himself when he can do me no service by it?"

should send into it 225 able and armed men for
soldiers, and, says Dr. Brown, "we find from entries
in the governor's letter book that these and subse-
quent orders were complied with." In another place
the governor remarks, "Bedfordshire men make a
faire show and tell them strange things." Quite lately
the muster rolls of this Newport garrison have been
brought to light, and from these it appears that John
Bunyan served in the Parliamentary army and was at
Newport for over two years and a half, Sir Samuel
Luke being in command of the garrison. Bunyan
was first in Col. Cockayne's Company (the Cockaynes
were Cardington people, neighbours of Sir Samuel
Luke); afterwards he was transferred to the company
of Col. Chas. O'Hara.

Running over the names in these rolls one wonders
who amongst them were drafted from this neighbourhood. There are several familiar Harrold names of the
time: Fleming, Ward, Odell, Saunders, Paull, the
latter being, we may conjecture, a descendant
of our esteemed vicar, the Rev. Robt. Paull. But
whoever the Harrold recruits may have been, at
Newport they would meet, and probably some of
them would converse with the tinker youth the
sound of whose name in after years was to go forth

into all lands. Bunyan was drafted into the army the very day he reached the statute age, sixteen. He was born on the 30th Nov., 1628, and on the 30th Nov., 1644, his name appears on the roll of Col. Cockayne's Company.*

Another important personage that our Harrold recruits would meet with was the eldest and most promising son of Oliver Cromwell. He, it appears, served under Sir Samuel Luke at Newport, and died there of small pox. A civil young gentleman, as the papers of the time said, and the joy of his father.

I said just now that "Bedfordshire sided with the Parliament." There were three counties in England, all of whose members, for borough and county alike, were on the side of Hampden and Pym, and Bedfordshire was one of the three, the other two

*It is worthy of note. and it shows how thoroughly Dr. Brown had looked up the evidence, and how clearly he saw the point towards which the converging rays seemed to tend, that years before the discovery of these muster rolls he divined the exact truth with regard to Bunyan's connection with the army. After discussing the arguments advanced in support of the contention that Bunyan enlisted in the Royalist Army, Dr. Brown says, "It is much more probable that as soon as he had reached the regulation age of sixteen he was included in one of the levies made by Parliament upon the villages of Bedfordshire, and without any choice of his own was sent, with others of his neighbours, to the important garrison of Newport." It is not often that conjecture is found to agree so closely with fact.

being Essex and Middlesex. The county thus being practically of one mind did not suffer from the civil war like some other counties. Lord St. John fell while leading his Bedfordshire recruits, but that was at Edgehill, near Banbury. Cannon balls have been found in the meadows below Odell Castle, proving that there must have been firing in the neighbourhood at some time, but there was in the county no regular seige or engagement.

Here, as elsewhere, of course, there was an absence of settled order; this is reflected in the register, which, for many years, appears to have been kept by the sexton, or anybody with any kind of ink and any kind of pen. During the *régime* of the Stuarts, church affairs were altogether unsettled. Nobody felt in safe possession, and nobody took any pride in the church or anything pertaining to it. Still things were not so bad here as in some places. At Woburn the curate was charged with baiting a bear in the church, at Knotting the rector and churchwardens were cited because that, on three successive Shrove Tuesdays, they "permitted, and were present at, cockfightings in the chancell of the said church, in or about the sacred place where the communion table stands, many persons being there assembled, and wagers laid." In later years the rector of Carlton was presented, because " immediately before service he did lead his horse in at the south doore into the chancell of Carlton church where he sett him and there continued all the time of the said service and sermon."*

On from the Restoration there is little to interest us besides a few wills which are satisfactory inasmuch as they show that people here had something to leave.

I have said that one of the de Greys took his title of earl from this village. His full title was the right honourable Anthony Lord Lucas Duke of Kent and Earl of Harrold, and he met with his death in 1723 under rather tragical circumstances. Passing through a harvest field at Silsoe, a beard of barley or something of the kind, which he inadvertently put in his mouth, stuck in his throat and choked him. In the Bedford Library is a copy of the funeral sermon preached by his Chaplain in St. Paul's Church before the Corporation and gentry of the county. Preachers and authors, a century or two ago, were sufficiently obsequious in the presence of the great, but making due allowance, it would seem that this Earl of Harrold

---

*" John Bunyan, his life, times, and work," by John Brown, B.A., D.D.

must have been a man of really exceptional excellence. "He knew," says the preacher, "all that belonged to his rank without assuming it. Perhaps there never was a more convincing instance that where men have real worth the not insisting on all that is due to them gives them abundantly the more." "He was far from thinking that because his condition set him above the necessity of labour he was only to divert and amuse himself." The sentiment underlying this extract is worthy of all acceptation. A man may perhaps begin to think about living altogether to or for himself when he is able to provide altogether for himself.

This Anthony, Earl of Harrold, married a sister of the Honourable Mrs. Ann Joliffe, whose effigy in marble is to be seen in the chancel of the church. By her will, dated Aug. 4, 1723, only a fortnight after her brother-in-law, the earl, met with his death, she devised an estate at Odell towards the erection of almshouses and the subsistence of widows to be placed in such almshouses. Her niece, Mrs. Mead, the daughter of Sir Rowland Alston, she appointed sole executrix with orders to buy ground and erect other almshouses so as to make them up to six.* The

---

*These last three are built on a parcel of the close called Wellocks.

widows in these almshouses receive weekly, I believe, one loaf, and ten shillings yearly for fuel.

Mrs. Mead was the wife of Dr. Mead, a very famous physician who, for a time, lived at Harrold Hall, and whose portrait hangs in the Reading Room of the Bedford Library. She also became a benefactor of Harrold; by her will in 1736 she bequeathed land, the annual rental of which then was £34 8s. od. £20 a year of this was to go to the clergyman for a Sunday afternoon lecture or service, the remainder to be spent in the purchase of bread and firewood for the poor, and in the repairing of the almshouses.

Two years afterwards, in 1738, Anthony Clarke devised land, the rent of which, £3 a year, was to be given to the poor in the form of bread and bull beef. The same year, Ann Franklin, by deed, conveyed land producing £6 a year for the benefit of the poor and £100 in money, the interest on which was to go to the clergyman. This charity is lost, the deed at some time having been intentionally destroyed.

In 1761 some person unknown left £15 in money, the interest on which was to be given, at the direction of the overseers, to the poor not receiving help out of the rates.

It is rather curious that all these benefactions were given about the same time. It seems as though there must have been an epidemic of benevolence just then. For fifty years it prevailed, then it died out, nobody has caught it since. Had it persisted down to the present day what abundance of charity there would have been now to distribute! With so much to be got for nothing nobody here would have needed to do much. Harrold would have been a very sanatorium for those suffering from Mr. Jerome's distressing malady—a disinclination for all kinds of work. We should only, all of us, have had to come here, declare ourselves needy persons, and bread and coal and blankets would have been supplied us without our being under the disagreeable necessity of having to work for such things.

Harrold has fewer charities than some villages; perhaps, though, there are enough. It is nice to see worthy old people, veterans from the great army of workers, provided for, but, beyond a certain limit, charity does more harm than good. In Italy and other places on the continent, where almsgiving is regarded as a cardinal virtue, beggars abound so as to be a pest. In this country we are trying another, a more excellent way. By extending political and

social privileges we are aiming to get things so that
every man may have a chance to provide for himself
and family without being under obligation to anybody.

Whether we ever attain to it or no, this I maintain
is a noble ideal, and I cannot but think we are moving
towards it though with slow, assuredly, and erratic
steps. Think of our noble benefit societies, the Odd
Fellows, the Foresters, the Free Gardeners, and others
(numbering altogether some 3,000,000 members) all
built up and kept going by working men. Why, in
our small town of Bedford, over four thousand
working-men voluntarily tax themselves, so that in
sickness and at death they may be independent of
extraneous help. More than some other things we
boast of these benefit societies are a sublime fact, a
monument of self-reliance, of which any nation may
well be proud. One often feels tempted to ask
whether our civilisation is anything other than beating
time to changing tunes, but I always feel comforted
and take fresh courage when I think of our noble
benefit societies, and the way working-men manage
them. Mind, this is no argument for *laisser faire*, no
apology for close-fistedness. There will never be a
lack of good people and good causes needing and
deserving help ; the only question is in what way we

can best use or leave our money so as to help people above the need of help. There are one or two things wanted badly in this village, a room, for instance, for young people to turn into of an evening. If anybody here wants to die and do a good deed, instead of almhouses I would say try something calculated to make ordinary life brighter and worthier; endow a public hall for reading, music, drill, and similar elevating recreations, something after the pattern of the Hawkins' Memorial Hall, on the Queen's Park Estate, at Bedford, and which is answering so well.

Besides the register the only other parish records are the churchwardens' account books and the *Award* of the Enclosure Commissioners. From the former, which dates back to 1759, I find that a mole-catcher used to be employed at a salary of £2 a year; after the regular office was abolished the authorities continued paying twopence for every mole taken to them, and do so, I believe, still. It was the same with cock robin's murderer—the pert, pilfering sparrow. Year after year are entries of considerable sums paid for sparrows. The reward for a fox, or a fox's head was a shilling,

The ringers, on special occasions, used to receive 2s. 6d. In some places the account reads: 2s. 6d. for beer for ringers, only beer is spelt "bear." One entry is rather amusing, it reads thus: "For ringers, on the execution of Tom Paine, 5s." This was in 1792, the year of the French Revolution. At that time Paine was in France, under arrest, and it was reported that he was shot; so the Vicar or Churchwardens, it seems, determined now that the arch heretic was out of the way to have a double bob peal. As it proved, however, Paine was not executed, but came over to England again, and died some years after.* When the news reached Harrold of Nelson's great victory at the Nile, there must have been a grand holiday, for the ringers then received 12s. 6d., or five times the ordinary fee.†

The half-acre strips, which originally comprised a villein's holding, were, as I have before said, not all together, but were distributed here and there all over three arable fields. This arrangement, as the village economy became less communistic, was found to be exceedingly inconvenient, and, besides that, a great

---

*We cannot say, for certain, that the ringers, when the error was discovered, returned the 5s. It does not, at any rate, appear in the accounts.

†One of these churchwardens must have been "a fair nailer." I see that he got some one to engage to clean the church clock and keep it in good going order for 2s. 6d. a year.

deal of the land was common and consequently was not cultivated by anybody. Even so late as the lattter part of the last century three-fourths of the land in Bedfordshire was unenclosed common land.

To remedy this state of things commissioners were appointed to arrange exchanges of land and to enclose the waste. Three Commissioners were appointed for Harrold in 1797, just a century ago, and the result of their labours is to be seen in the *Award of Harrold*. The particulars of that award, however, would take too much time to go into. I can only say generally that, besides effecting exchanges for the convenience of owners of property, and awarding all the common lands except the village green, they also defined the public highways and footpaths. Following upon the appointment of these commissioners an Act was passed in 1802 for making a turnpike road from Great Staughton to Sharnbrook, thence on through Odell and Harrold to Lavendon.

With regard to footpaths, Harrold is very fortunate in having so many. I hope Harrold people will see to it that no usurper ever robs them of any one of them. When my daughter lived at Rose Villa it was a great pleasure to me to go out backway, over the little plank bridge, then on to the stile by the hedge, and to find footpaths radiating thence in almost every direction. I deduce from this convenience of footpaths that the lords of the Manor at Harrold have been on the whole a kindly and not over-reaching race.

The Commissioners for Harrold were Joseph Pawsey, of Silsoe; John Davis, of Bloxham, Oxfordshire; and George Maxwell, of Spalding, Lincolnshire. For their services they received two guineas a day, paying their own expenses. The deed authorising them sets forth that: "Whereas, in the parish of Harrold, in the county of Bedford, there are certain common and open fields, meadows, and waste grounds, containing, together, 3,300 acres, or thereabouts," these commissioners were to appoint a time for receiving applications from proprietors respecting the situations where they would prefer to have their allotments.

Of the arable land, they were to allot one-fifth to the church, in lieu of tithe,* together with one-ninth of the sward and commons, and one-tenth of the woods and spinnies. The lord of the Manor was to have one-twentieth of the waste lands; all other

---

*The rectorial estate now consists principally of Harrold Lodge Farm.

claims and exchanges were to be settled at the dis-
cretion of the commissioners, and a copy of the
valuation had to be lodged at the *Wheat Sheaf* for
public inspection. As boundaries, the commissioners
almost everywhere recommended or insisted on the
planting of quick-set hedges, and have thereby much
enhanced the general beauty of the country.

Down to the time of George the Third, every
person who moved from his native place to another
village had to take with him a certificate from the
overseers or churchwardens to show what place he
belonged to, then if he came to need relief he had to
go back to his own parish ; if he was unable to walk
he was sent back in a cart or other conveyance. Of
these certificates there is a large number in the parish
chest.   I give one as a specimen : —

*Certificate of Forty Aresum.—We, Tobias Dally, John
Beall, Thomas Allen and William Rodgers, church-
wardens and overseers of the poor of the parish of
Wellingborough in the county of Northampton do hereby
own and acknowledge Forty Aresum, periwig maker, and
Mary his wife, now residing at Harrold, in the county of
Bedford, to be inhabitants legally settled in the parish of
Wellingborough aforesaid.   In witness whereof we hereby
subscribe our names — — Dated April 20th, 1747.*

Several wealthy people about this time were living at Harrold, and so this Forty Aresum, who, we may suppose, had not been doing very well at Wellingborough, came to try his fortune here. Unfortunately for him, periwigs just then were going out of fashion and the succeeding fashion of pigtails, though quite elaborate as compared with our fashion or absence of fashion to-day, involved nothing like such a business as the making of periwigs. The old archers used to say, "Be sure to have more than one string to your bow"; our hairdresser's second string was the cleaning and repairing of clocks. In the churchwarden's book are entries of several small sums paid to him for repairing the church clock. A year or two after Aresum came to Harrold he had a son, who was christened Forty after his father. It is an odd name, Forty Aresum. It must have been, I should think, a corruption of a French name.

Besides this periwig maker various other craftsmen, I find by these certificates, settled here at one time or another: Stephen Morris, parchment maker; Joshua Harris, collar maker; Edward Abrahams (from Olney), stay maker. Neither of these businesses, we may assume, took very deep root here; the trade which has come, as we say, to stay, is that of leather dressing. This was introduced about fifty years ago by a Mr. Edward Rate, a fell monger. Whilst carrying on his business at Odell, a dyer from London came past, seeking employment. The wayfaring man seemed to be smart and intelligent, so Mr. Rate took him on and soon set about turning the information the man had to impart to practical account. Afterwards, having some dispute with his landlord, he moved to Harrold. So began the Harrold leather trad,e the first shop or premises being where Mr. W. Manton now lives. Fortunately there was in the village intelligence and enterprise to follow up the start thus made. Now there are four firms, employing altogether nearly a hundred hands, a very large proportion for a village, indeed, considering its size, Harrold, I believe, is quite a leading place in this branch of trade.

Well would it be if small industries could be introduced into most of our villages, to save them from depopulation and decay. Our children's toys and many of the nicknacks that are supposed to embellish our rooms were made in Bavarian villages. Why should we, in our villages, be dependent entirely upon the land and be all the while losing all the best parts of our population?

It is this leather trade, no doubt, which, to a large extent, accounts for the air of comparative comfort and prosperity which a visitor cannot but notice here. An outward and visible sign of this prosperity, I often think, is to be seen on Sundays. I don't mean the Sunday finery, though that is something wonderful. No, I mean the dinners which, as you go from church or chapel, you see so many people taking home from the bakehouse. It is usually a small joint set on a tripod over a Yorkshire pudding, a humble affair, nothing very Epicurean about it, yet how briskly do the bearers trip along, how carefully do they hold it, and how lovingly do they look at it. Sunday labour! Well, we will not go into that controversy. I am glad, at any rate, that so many in Harrold are in a position to now and then get something better than pork dumpling, toad in the hole as it is facetiously called. I greatly believe in a weekly change: it is altogether wholesome for a man, one day a week, to lay aside corduroy and invest himself in a Sunday suit, and if with the better raiment he can get better food, why then, say I, so much the better.

A STROLL THROUGH THE VILLAGE.

A Stroll through the Village.

FROM almost the beginning of the Christian Era we have made our way somehow down through the past; here we are now in the present. Before, however, we part company and bid each other adieu, suppose we take a stroll through the village, and see what else we can glean of its history from its buildings. For a starting point we cannot do better than go as far as the bridge. Being narrow, it has recesses, so that people at night can get out of the way of passing vehicles. According to an old story, a Duke of Portland, in his carriage, once met a countryman with a cart on a narrow bridge. Neither would back out for the other to pass; at last the Duke, with threatening voice and gesture, said, "Look here, if you don't back out of my way I'll serve you as I did a fellow awhile ago." The man, a little intimidated, backed out, and afterwards asked him what he did to the other fellow. "Oh," said the Duke, laughing, "as he wouldn't get out of my way I got out of his."

he piers of the bridge are very massive, too massive;

they not only obstruct the floodwater, but they cause a lot of sediment to be deposited. The islands above and below the bridge are doubtless due to these wide and massive piers.

The most cursory inspection shows that it is very old ; the first stone bridge in England was built, it is said, by order of Queen Matilda in 1126. This bridge, we know by the Hundred Rolls, cannot be much less ancient; most likely it was built in place of an earlier wooden structure. It is inconceivable that an engineering people like the Romans should be about here for three or four hundred years collecting tribute mainly in the form of produce, and yet not have thrown a bridge of some kind over the river.

Trailing away from the bridge towards Carlton is the causeway, Harrold pier I call it, dad's pier my people call it, because I so often take my pleasure there walking to and fro. It is nearly 300 yards long by about ten feet wide and six feet above the roadway. When I first came to Harrold, I enquired about this causeway, and was credibly informed that it was made originally by the Romans. This account I received with ready unquestioning faith. Imagine my dismay, when, after living in this assurance five or six years, I was told by some wiseacre that it is quite a modern work!

Now I have walked this causeway at nearly all hours. In the early morning I have seen the prodigious flights of starlings literally darkening the sky; the heron sailing majestically high overhead; the wild ducks keeping an almost geometrical pattern as they flew past calling to one another. In the daytime, looking around, I have often thought what a lovely pastoral view you get there, reminding you of some of the Dutch landscapes.

I have been there at night, too, when the sky has been strewn with stars, "the floor of Heaven" as Shakspeare puts it "thick inlaid with patines of bright gold" and from there as an observatory I have traced the constellations and told the stars—Orion with studded belt, Arcturus, Capella, Sirius, Vega, the planets, too, with the silver crescent moon. Then, looking down as I moved slowly along, I seemed to see those Roman pioneers busy laying the foundation stones of the causeway seventeen centuries ago. At such times the place seemed a sort of holy ground, and now to be told that it is quite a modern work carried out by Navvy, Mason and Co., contractors, at a cost of so much a cubic yard!

Now I am not going to say confidently that the causeway is Roman, but I do say that it cannot be " quite a modern work." If you look underneath you will find that some of the arches are encrusted with a considerable thickness of stalactite, a deposit which even in limestone caves, where the ooze is constant, is formed almost inconceivably slowly. In Lyson's " Bedfordshire," published in 1806, the causeway is mentioned, and in Fisher's sketches of about the same time it looks much as it does now. The cement used looks like Roman, some of the more ancient looking archstones being cemented so that no wedge or chisel could ever split them across the joints. The spirit of the work, if I may so speak, is not at all modern. If you want to see how such work has been carried out in modern times you have an example at Felmersham—the plank bridge. " The ancients," says Mr. Hughes, C. E., " substituted quantity for quality ; their bridges consisted of a long low series of culverts, hardly deserving the name of arches, with intervening piers often of greater thickness than the span of the arches they were built to support." This passage describes exactly the architecture of both these structures. Harrold causeway must have been built by people, whether Romans or

Normans, who were in the habit of building massive stone structures, massive even to a fault.

Going from the bridge we pass the entrance gate to the hall, on which is to be seen the crest of the Alstons, " an estoile or in a crescent arg." in plain language, a gold star over a silver crescent with the curious motto "*Immotus*." Here most probably was the manor house of feudal times, the mansion of Gilbert de Blosseville, the tenant or vicegerent of Judith. From him the property passed to the De Greys, Ralph Morin in the thirteenth century holding it under their " superiority." During the reigns of Edward II. and III., the Hastings, who were related to the De Greys, were the leading family in Harrold; later, in the time of Edward VI., Thos. Cheyne or Cheyney, a son probably of John Cheyney, gent., to whom Henry gave part of the spoils of the Priory, was resident here. By his will, among other dispositions of his property, he says " I gyve to everye house in Harrold that hath not a plough going, a bushell of malt, also I give to the reparations of the bridge in Harrold, xls ; and I give to all godchildren in Harrold to each of them iiijs."

About this time, or soon after, a branch or offshoot of the Botelers, of Biddenham, got settled here. The

Botelers' family place was the old mansion house at
Ford End. In 1643 a marriage was projected between
George Orlebar, of Harrold, and Ursula Boteler,
daughter of Oliver Boteler, of Biddenham. George's
mother, Margaret, had seventeen children, of whom
he was the eldest.   Ursula's mother was daughter of
Thomas Hawes, Alderman of Bedford, the founder,
I believe, of the Hawes Charity. A brass to his
memory is to be seen in St. Mary's Church, Bedford.
The Botelers, too, were a prolific race; there must
have been a number of them at Harrold, for the name
occurs frequently in the early pages of the register.
Butler is supposed to be the modern form of the name.
The head of the family here was Sir Thomas Boteler.
Sir Thomas, it would seem, must have been popular,
for at least one in every four of the boys born
in the village about this time was christened
" Thomas."

In the first half of the 17th century four families of
title were living at Harrold: the Botelers, the Orlebars
from Hinwick, the Dudleys from Rutland or North-
amptonshire, and the Farrers from Brayfield. The
Bletsoes, too, were living here about the same
time. The Dudleys came to Harrold in 1618; they
probably built the residence called the Mansion,

now occupied by Mr. John Fairey. The date 1619 is conspicuous on the chimney outside. The mansion is a well designed and substantially-built structure, the studded front door being particularly interesting. Memorial stones to members of these various families are to be seen in the church. That so many people of position should be living here together is further proof that Harrold, in past times, was a leading village in the hundred.

The Alstons only came to this neighbourhood towards the end of the 16th century. According to Cooper, the historian of Odell, they are presumably of Saxon origin, "as may be gathered from the name, which, in that language, signifies most noble or excellent." The present mansion was built originally in the form of the letter E, but the southern recess was filled in by a new building, comprising a large drawing room and dining room, with bedrooms over. These additions were made in 1816 by Sir Thomas Alston, the grandfather of the present proprietor.

Now let us go through the little gateway, and along the path towards the church. On our left is the fine avenue of venerable limes leading up to the hall. From the tree-tops, thickly crowded with nests;

the voices of the rooks can be heard in the land
" cawing and jawing " all the day long.   The lime,
it is said, was the chosen tree of the Roundheads, as
the pine latterly was of the Cavaliers.   One wonders
whether these limes were meant by some Cromwel-
lian tenant of the hall to serve as a memorial.

The church is of composite architecture—Transition
Norman, Early English and Decorated.   How old is
it ?   We may almost as well ask how old is the village;
from the very introduction of Christianity in most
towns and villages there have been places of worship
of some sort, and a church, as we see it, is but the
latest example of a succession of renovations.   The
spire and windows are decorated, and that style had
not developed till about the year 1300, but some
parts of the structure tell of a Norman edifice, and
there would almost certainly be a rude Saxon church
or moot hall before that.   The list of known vicars
numbers 46 ; the first was named Walter, the second
Eudo, the third Willm de Bukingham.   With one
doubtful exception the late vicar, the Rev. John
Steel, M.A., held the living longer than any
predecessor.   Thomas Bazeley, who was vicar in
1792, published a volume of sermons, also a work
called " *The Glory of the Heavens:*"   His successor,

Robert Woodward, was the author of a pamphlet on " *The Errors of the Dissenters, illustrative of the erroneous pretences for separation from the Ancient Established Church.*" This pamphlet was printed at Bedford, and a copy is in the General Library. The most striking monument in the church is that in the chancel to the Honourable Dame Anne Joliffe. The silver paten was the gift of this lady, the flagon of her sister, the Hon. Lady Temperance Wolstenholme, in 1726.

The church has five bells. The first bears the inscription ·" 1608, Prais the Lord"; 2nd, " 1603, Cum, Cum, and Praye"; 3rd, " 1652, Chandler Made Me"; 4th, " 1678, John Hudson, of Landon, Made Mee"; 5th, " 1756, Thomas Knight and William Wootton Made Me."* When the steeple was repaired in 1826, a tom-tit's nest, with four eggs in it, was found in the cavity of the weather-cock. The spindle, on which the weather-cock turned, had worn the hole so large as to leave room for the little tom-tit to pass in and out.

Going now from the church towards the village

---

*Since the above was written the bells have been tuned and re-hung, and a sixth bell added by Messrs. Taylor, of Loughborough.

one can see by the architecture that there was, at one time, a fine house at the back of the rectory. It was built by Francis Farrer, Esq., about 1690. After his death it was occupied by his widow, then by the Hon. Lady Wolstenholme. This lady's first husband was Sir Rowland Alston, by whom she had thirteen children.* After his death, while her son, Sir Thomas Alston, was on his travels, she built the largest part of the present Odell mansion, the south front, 105 feet long, on the site of the ancient castle keep. Afterwards she married Sir John Wolstenholme, Bart., of Enfield Middlesex, a widower, who also, says Cooper, had a family of thirteen. Upon the death of her second husband, Lady Wolstenholme came and lived here at Harrold. She and Dame Joliffe were daughters of Lord Crewe : consequent upon their relationship with the Alstons, several members of the latter family have since borne the name of Crewe.

After Lady Wolstenholme, the mansion was tenanted by a Dr. Payne, and after him by the Rev. Mr. Taylor. Finally it was converted into three or four small tenements, but the arms of the Farrers,

*According to the tablet in Odell church this lady had fourteen children, eight sons and six daughters.

OLD MANSION OF THE FARRERS.

From FISHER'S "Sketches of Bedfordshire."

the original owners, are still to be seen, carved in oak, above Miss Houghton's fireplace. Outside, on the front of the building, is an ancient sundial bearing the motto, *Ecce Fugio.*

From this ancient mansion we go on to the modern one of Mr. Pettit, which was built in 1886, Mr. John Day, of Bedford, being the architect. It is a very fine house, and, since its erection, has, in various ways, been much improved. On the opposite side of the street are two villa residences, built a few years ago by Mr. Clayson. Harrold people evidently do not see why the towns should have a monopoly of architectural show and domestic convenience.

Proceed we now to the village green, which I wish was larger, more like that of Elstow or Goldington. Perhaps part of it was enclosed after the passing of the Enclosure Act, or possibly Harrold people have been always too busy for such games and frivolities as John Bunyan speaks of. The market place or shelter tells of the market which was formerly held here.* Having a market and petty sessions, Harrold then was a town, and town, I see, in Kelly's Directory, it is still called.

---

*By charter, probably about the beginning of the seventeenth century. — Harvey's " History of the Willey Hundred."

K

At the back of the shelter we come to the old round-house, one of the most notable relics in Harrold, for very few of these round-houses remain now in the country. One or two features about this structure I wish to direct your attention to. First, its architecture. Compare it with this rough sketch of a Bongo hut in Central Africa; when I showed the sketch during my former lecture nearly everybody thought it was meant for the round-house. Is it not strange that a style of architecture evidently so primitive should have persisted so long in a civilised country? The explanation probably is this:—in the realm of officialism changes are resisted as long as possible, or are adopted only very slowly and reluctantly. Where men are not induced or compelled by competition to move on they cling to old styles and ways till they become so out of date as to be ridiculous. Witness the wigs of judges, and the aprons and knee-breeches of bishops.

Then, again, look at the doorway, from sill to lintel it is barely 5 feet. The average height of Englishmen now is about 5 feet 8 inches, and they say, you know, that we are nothing like such fine fellows as Old England used to grow. Now why did they make their doorway so low? Why did they not make it so

THE ROUNDHOUSE.

Photo by W. R. FAIREY, HARROLD.

that the village reeve might really run his man in instead of having to almost double him up to get him in ? To this question, evolution, perhaps, furnishes the likeliest answer. The beehive hut of pre-historic times had for doorway a mere semi-circular hole, through which the dwellers crawled in or out on hands and knees. Gradually the beehive changed to the round-house, the round-house to the rectangular hovel. There was no abrupt transition, no jumping from the beehive hut to the modern cottage. Similarly with the openings or doorways, there was no sudden spring from 2 feet 6 inches to 6 feet 6 inches. Only by little and little could the builders free themselves from the spell, the bias of the past. To this day the influence of the beehive style of architecture is perceptible ; two or three of the older cottages in the village have doorways even lower than that of the round-house.

Close by, only a few yards to our right, is the village school, the site for which was conveyed to the vicar and churchwardens in 1847 by the right hon. the Earl de Grey. It is a voluntary school, in the management of which churchmen and dissenters seem to work harmoniously together. These two, the round house and the schoolhouse, standing side by side, may be regarded as types of the past and present; the one dark, damp, repulsive, representing a system altogether penal and vindictive, which charged upon the offender the whole blame of his offence as though he had made himself and all his surroundings; the other an expression of the growing feeling or sentiment that men and women do not altogether make themselves, but that if we are to have reputable citizens, society must see to it that the conditions are favourable for their growth. The former times we are sometimes told were better than these; such a conclusion is not to be deduced from these two instances.

Our way now leads past Mow hills on which the Priory once stood; to our right is the Mission Hall founded by the Misses St. Quintin, Mr. Croxford being the minister. The lane further on branching off from the main road is called Brook Lane, because a pretty brook runs down one side of it, the cottages on that side being approached by little arched bridges giving the place something, let us say, of a Venetian aspect. A few yards beyond the lane we come to the Congregational Chapel or Church, as the people prefer to call it. This church was planted by the society called the Bedfordshire Union of Christians about the year 1802. At first services were held in a temporary building, then in 1808 a chapel was erected which in 1836, and again in 1863, was considerably enlarged, and is now fully equipped with schoolroom and manse. In 1811 Mr. West, a student from Newport, was ordained as the first pastor. He was succeeded in 1827 by Mr. Phillips, a man much esteemed, who ministered here for thirty-four years. After Mr. Phillips, Dr. Deane, a D.Sc., and a man of some scientific repute, was here for about eight years. Following him came Mr. Skinner, B.A., then Mr. Jones to whom there is a tablet in the chapel; last came Mr. Martindale the esteemed president of your Society.

Harrold Congregationalists are to be complimented on their public spirit and the taste shown in the adornment of their place of worship. An old Puritan divine seriously maintained that starch was invented by the devil. Looking into the generality of village chapels it would seem that there must be a prevalent conviction abroad that the same shady personage invented paint also and varnish.

And now we have come to the end of what has been to me a pleasant, and to you, I hope, a not altogether unprofitable excursion. Most of the way we have come we could get only glimpses of what we wanted to see; still you have seen sufficient I hope to make you feel more interested in your native place. As you walk down your main street or from the bridge, watch the river flowing on and on you ought to feel somewhat of a thrill when you remember that the Romans trod this very ground eighteen hundred years ago, and that in later Saxon and feudal times Harrold was by no means the least among the villages of Bedfordshire.

It is too much the tendency just now to give up the village; people seem to tacitly agree that its day is gone by; the old order of agriculture has given way to the new of manufactures and commerce, and so the village is being abandoned like a partly exhausted working; as houses decay they are not repaired or rebuilt, but like professional cripples, are allowed to exhibit for years their sores and deformities to the passers by. In this respect Harrold differs from many; the process of decay is not allowed to go on unchecked; you see no reason why progress and improvement should be confined to towns; you have new houses here which would not be out of place in the most aristocratic part of Bedford. There is here, too, a pulsing of intellectual life and public spirit. By voluntary effort you light up your streets;

you have your annual flowershow, and your magazine
club. Now and then, you get up a concert or an
entertainment, which for display of talent I am told
is not to be despised; even this Mutual Society is a
sign, a symptom of healthy life. Go on. Set an
example worthy of being copied by others. Emulate
each other in your gardens and window plants.* In
cleanliness and general appearance let it be your
pride to make your village a model unto many.

You see what has been done at Turvey and Warden;
be it yours to emulate even to better these examples.
As things are it cannot be expected that a Higgins
or a Shuttleworth will spring up in every village; be
yours the better part to show what can be done by
the free healthy spirit of the many working together
for the general well-being and enjoyment. Every
man's concern with the place where he lives has
something more in it, says Toulmin Smith, than the
mere amount of rates and taxes he has to pay. If
you have made money here don't move off to some big
town where you will be only one very small star in a
firmament; let your money circulate in and benefit
your own neighbourhood. My own experience is
that whether as regards investments or benefactions,

---

*I noted the cottages at one end of the village as I went past.
Out of forty-eight I found that forty-two have plants in the
windows.

it is unwise to let much of your money go very far out of your sight. If you want to leave money for a public purpose, leave it as a fund for your parish council to use for the improvement of the village as they may from time to time see occasion. As a beginning they might pave the causeway with flags; then if you were to put a few seats along and could arrange to have all your floods together in the latter part of the summer, you would have your seaside at home !

Seriously, I believe it would *pay* to renovate and beautify a village here and there. Quiet people are getting weary of fashionable holiday resorts with their vulgar swagger and pretence. Even as regards fashionable places abroad, like Paris, many when they sit down afterwards to count up the cost, ask themselves ruefully what they have got for all the expense. A Devonshire lane, says Grant Allen, is worth ten thousand Palais Royals. You have no lack of pleasant scenery and velvety footpaths, and if you can see your way to improve your causeway, as I suggest, it would be a great attraction.

In conclusion, if what I have so imperfectly said shall quicken your interest in your native place, I shall feel that I have done something in return for the many happy restful hours I have spent here ; quiet rural joys, courtesies, too, and kindnesses, the remembrance of which will not soon pass away.

Lightning Source UK Ltd.
Milton Keynes UK
UKHW031507090223
416681UK00013B/2964